SURF
RAGE

JOLI

MARTIN TULLEMANS

JOLI

Above: *Who had the right of way? The surfer on the inside?
The one paddling first? The one waiting the longest? There has
always been a big crew in the line up at Waimea Bay, most times
sanity prevails and it's one surfer one wave, which is much safer
on giant waves.*

Opposite top: *With so many forms of surf craft what is needed
is more tolerance by all of us, especially in crowded conditions.*
Opposite below: *One of the alternatives to Surf Rage, man-made
waves. This is Tom Lochtefeld's classic standing wave.*

Page 1: *More than one surfer riding the same wave is potentially
very dangerous. Jason and Josh at Rocky Point on Oahu, in Hawaii.*

JOLI

Above: *The surfer on the inside is the talented Hawaiian local David Miller. Dave obviously took off on this wave first and is trying desperately to get around this kid who's dropped in and created this ugly situation.*

Opposite: *The comic consequences of overcrowding.*

G.C.B. *PhotoCopy*

Gold Coast
Bulletin

Sydney 2000
OFFICIAL PARTNER

Monday, February 28, 2000
70 By Air Extra

Phone 5539 2522
Classifieds 5597 8000

Who will run with our torch bearers

POLL TIPS:
BAILDON LANDSLIDE
● Page 4

Full list of Olympic escorts
● Pages 30-31

Surf rage

Tempers dump on sporting image

The Gold Coast's Trudy Todd (above) and junior champ Samantha Cornish (inset)

by GREG STOLZ and
LARA FRAWLEY

THE Gold Coast's world No 3 surfer Trudy Todd has been fined and faces suspension from next month's Billabong Pro after an altercation at a major women's tournament at Snapper Rocks.

Todd yesterday admitted pushing a young competitor's head into the sand after she was eliminated.

Officials and spectators said they were shocked by the incident, involving grommet and eventual winner Samantha Cornish.

The dust-up comes amid a weekend of 'surf rage' with one suspension and several violent incidents at the Queensland Surf Life Saving State Titles at North Kirra.

Todd yesterday defended her actions

saying she retaliated over an incident in the water as part of an ongoing feud between the two.

"The facts are that she was hassling the hell out of me out in the water – I told her off. She shoved me and I just put her head in the sand," said Todd.

"People saw me push her head into the sand and her crying and assumed I was at fault but that's not the case at all. It was not grommet bashing."

● See 24-page sports liftout
● Continued Page 2

Karla could miss the Nationals

6

Above: *The disastrous consequences of Surf Rage.*

Following page: *The original tribal law plaque from Margaret River, Western Australia. Conceived and brought to fruition by Robert Conneeley, Rosco Kermode and Peter Cuming.*

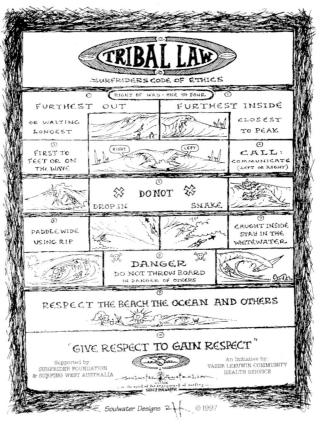

TRIBAL LAW
SURFRIDERS CODE OF ETHICS

RIGHT OF WAY : ONE TO FOUR

FURTHEST OUT	FURTHEST INSIDE
OR WAITING LONGEST	CLOSEST TO PEAK
FIRST TO FEET OR ON THE WAVE	CALL: COMMUNICATE (LEFT OR RIGHT)

RIGHT · LEFT

DO NOT DROP IN · SNAKE

| PADDLE WIDE USING RIP | CAUGHT INSIDE STAY IN THE WHITEWATER |

DANGER
DO NOT THROW BOARD
IN DANGER OF OTHERS

RESPECT THE BEACH THE OCEAN AND OTHERS

"GIVE RESPECT TO GAIN RESPECT"

Supported by:
SURFRIDER FOUNDATION
& SURFING WEST AUSTRALIA

An Initiative by:
VASSE LEEUWIN COMMUNITY
HEALTH SERVICE

Soulwater Australia
... in the spirit of the enjoyment of surfing ...
SHARE THE WATER

Soulwater Designs © 1997

AN IDEA BORN IN THE WATERS OF MARGARET RIVER.

the "Tribal Law - Surfriders Code of Ethics" is a community
developed project aimed at reducing surf related injuries
and encouraging the return of 'RESPECT' amoungst surfers. A
project endorsed by leading Community, Business, Environmental
and Sporting groups, it requires only one more supporter...

you...

WE ARE VERY LUCKY TO BE SURFERS – SHARE THE WATER

Soulwater Australia
2.H. ©97

SURF RAGE

NAT YOUNG

NYMBOIDA PRESS

Special thanks to the San Diego police prosecutor and surfer Steve Anear.

The events, opinions and feelings expressed and people mentioned by the
twelve individual authors of the chapters contained herein were written by
the individual authors from their own knowledge and research and compiled
into the final manuscript supplied to the publisher. The publisher and the
authors, consultants and editors expressly disclaim all and any liability and
responsibility to any person, whether a reader of this publication or not, in
respect of anything and of the consequences of anything done by any such
person in reliance, whether wholly or partially, upon the whole or any part
of the contents of this publication.

First published in 2000 by Nymboida Press, 8 Bay Street, Angourie, NSW,
2464 Australia.

National Library of Australia Cataloguing in Publication data:

Surf rage.

ISBN 0 9585750 1 0

1. Violence in sports – Australia. 2. Anger – Anecdotes.
3. Surfing – Australia. 4. Surfers – Assaults against –
Australia – Anecdotes. I. Young, Nat, 1947–

797.320994

Design and production by John Witzig & Co, Mullumbimby,
NSW, 2482, Australia.

Cover design by Graeme Murdoch.

Edited and proof read by Drew Kampion, Campbell Rielly and Tim Learner.

Printed in Singapore by PH Productions Pte Ltd.

CONTENTS

FOREWORD

Territory by Drew Kampion

Drew Kampion is 56 years young, he has been editor of SURFER *magazine, contributing editor of* SURFING MAGAZINE, *and editorial director of* WIND SURF *magazine. Drew lives with his family in Washington State, USA. He has been the author of numerous books and stories during his 45 years of involvement with the ocean.*

Surfing is something like a smorgasbord. We come to the table to indulge our appetites. Some of us act restrained, try to be fair. We are not first in line, and we're careful to leave the sundry offerings more or less intact for those who will follow us. Others enjoy an all-you-can-eat mindset, rushing to the food, heaping their plates to overflowing, dropping stuff left and right as they stagger off with pig grins and slavering noises to shovel it away as fast as possible so they can get back in line.

I stopped eating at places like the Viking's Trough, the Golden Wheelbarrow, and the Burst Bowel years ago. It wasn't just the food quality, it was that oppressive feeling of being in a place where too much greed was too freely circulating. It made me queasy, especially when I found myself enthusiastically sharing in the debauch, vaguely haunted by visions of starving (fill in a nationality here).

It's that same feeling out in the lineup as the hungry pack stalks the next set. Like desperate smorgasboarders [sic.] waiting for the next tray of stroganoff to arrive, there is no "we" here, just a bunch of primordial I's. Everyone wants first dibs, everyone wants the best slice of swell – a prime cut with no-one else trying to slide a piece of shoulder off their plate. "Hey, kook! MY BEEF!"

Like many, I dine elsewhere. Some days, at some surf spots, you get no respect for just being human, you get no respect unless you're very good or very bad – like evil bad. Evil gets all kinds of respect. Show me an evil surfer, and I'll show you a wave hog. The worst are the GOOD wave hogs. Man, they've got the power, and they know it. They get all the waves, and I just watch. It's their territory. If I drop in, him and his buds will NOT let that stand, nor will they GIVE me a wave. But, man, I'm hungry. "Maybe I should find some place else to surf. Maybe that new artificial reef. But jeez! There's a hundred guys out!"

Perhaps we COULD simply begin manufacturing artificial reefs at an alarming rate, something like 13 per day, create lots more territory. But would even this be enough? Doubtful. Nature abhors a damn vacuum, and humans (because of their so-called free will) do not distribute themselves evenly, like a gas. Instead, they collect at the world's honey pots, like bees. Build 13 artificial reefs a day, and 13,000 people a day will take up surfing. Just watch.

By the year 2025, the average surf session might well consist of 1.7 rides per surfer per session. For modern surfers, crowds simply come with the territory, and the territory is finite. Yesteryear's secret Mexican points are today's South Pacific reef passes. As globalised surf-consciousness lures millions to the ancient Polynesian pastime, just about every little nook and cranny will be surfed, publicised, and popularised.

Trying to stem this tide of surfing's popularity is fruitless. "The lady doth protest too much, methinks," says Hamlet. It's the same with every surfer "claiming" his or her territory. We'll just have to cope. Come to grips with the situation. Contemplate the forces at work. Understand the situation here – the friend, the foe, the ebb, the flow, the history.

Most indigenous peoples around the world were pitifully ignorant about personal territory until the Europeans taught them the principles of ownership. "Hey, thou ignorant savage! Relinquish that nail! It belongeth not to you!" Bang! Bang!

The principle of ownership – the idea of private personal territory – has been midwifed to its logical modern glory by generations of greed mongers, until today, if you buy a piece of property, you generally get the right to destroy every living thing upon it. For instance, I live in the Pacific Northwest of the USA, where one of the big tourism draws is Washington State's so-called majestic Olympic Peninsula. Well, I can tell you, the Olympic Peninsula is, for the most part, the butt-ugliest place I've ever seen. It's been ravaged by slashers and clearcutters, and most of the ancient forest has been shipped to Japan and other places where it's apparently more highly valued, because our so-called National Forest Service sells the stuff for far less than it costs them to build the roads that allow these f---ers to haul the beautiful carcasses off to the mills. Talk about dumb greed.

But I digress. The thing is, what is the source of this idea that when something is "yours", you have the right to do whatever you want with it? Where does the idea of ownership come from? I mean, in a sense it's logical. I kill the beast, then you show up and want to eat it. It's mine, I tell you. You don't completely agree. So: I kill you, you kill me, winner eats the beast. It's the kind of simple, primal logic you used to encounter in Oxnard, California, and still do, I'm told, at other more or less notorious spots.

But this kind of territorial logic only makes sense on a certain scale. It is only logical on a certain level of consciousness. Fighting over a carcass, while ignoring an onrushing wildfire is patently stupid, and so is fighting over waves while our beaches erode or our access is being revoked or the world goes to hell in a handbasket. Whatever. Even more to the point: Fighting over waves at the expense of the quality of the surfing experience is an utterly bankrupt activity. Give it up. Please.

But those who jealously guard their privacy or exclusivity think otherwise. They believe – they feel – the same natural territorial instincts of other animals. They feel instinctive certainty that such-and-such spot is theirs. They feel instinctive certainty as they pressure some visiting kook out of the lineup, all the while oblivious to the monster tsunami draining the shore as it races toward the reef bringing oblivion to the petty realities of the line-up. Call this tsunami global warming, life out of balance, galloping consumption, technological imperialism, digital mayhem, global corporatisation, matrix or Apocalypse, or whatever – it's coming, and the entire petty illusion of personal territory will vanish.

We've got to look at waves, like everything else, including our personal time in this world, as a limited resource. But with a difference. Waves are an UNLIMITED limited resource. The waves keep coming.

One of my favourite things about the 1960s was the way attitudes of ownership softened. There was an extant common realisation – something in the air – that any moment can be better for everybody – you, me, them – if we cooperate, share, and smile. I am not joking when I tell you that surfing was different in those days. There were smiles and conversations in the lineups, and surfers freely hooted as they watched others. Locals freely helped newcomers find the peak and catch a wave. It was bitchin', but all that faded away about the time the Hell's Angels bashed in some poor guy's head with pool cues at Altamont. The day the music died. The Rolling Stones always were the house band for the territorial paradigm.

When the hierarchy in the territory is corrupted by negativity, nothing good can come of it. When the organisation of the hierarchy is driven by instinctive emotions, there can be no real cohesion. The organisation of the hierarchy needs to be driven by a different principle; if it isn't, the territory will be lost.

INTRODUCTION

Nat Young

I'm sure no-one who has surfed Australia's Angourie Point on a good swell will dispute the fact that it is not an appropriate wave for a long board (or Malibu, as we call 'em Down Under). At Angourie, the wave jumps up very dramatically compared to a normal beachbreak wave; this sucking reef break really suits a shortboard, which can drop in later and steeper.

Another characteristic of Angourie is that when the swell has any angle from the east around to the north, the wave allows no room for cutting back, and the fetch at the base of the wave is very short and far too tight to accommodate the length and turning radius of a longboard. So, in order to take off on a wave with a longboard, you have to be facing away from the curl.

On 16 March 2000, my son Beau took off on a wave already occupied by a long board surfer named Michael Hutchison. A friend shouted for Beau (who was riding his short board) to go for it, that Michael would never make the wave. But Michael is a pretty good surfer, and he beats most waves he takes. I just happened to be at the end of that wave, and as Michael gave "stink-eye" to Beau for dropping in on him, I opened my big mouth, saying something to Beau about not worrying about Michael 'cause he does that to everyone. Michael kept paddling, but I knew he heard me. I could just feel him seething.

In fact, Michael Hutchison had been pissed at me for years, since the first time I met him, back when he was getting every set wave at The Point on his long board, while all the old blokes and kids were trying to take off on their short boards. Even so, I occasionally talked with him; in retrospect, I wish I had kept up the dialogue. It's vital to be vocal about how you're feeling, to tell the other person, even if it's a matter of telling 'em you're pissed off. Try to remember that there is nothing wrong with anger: it's the way you express the emotion that is so critical.

Anyway, things went on like that for a while, then a couple of years ago, in the course of conversation, Michael told me how much he respected me. Even so, he still took off on every set wave, something that isn't done according to the unspoken rules of surfing. But instead of telling him how I felt, I chose to leave the water whenever he paddled out. I honestly thought it was the best way to avoid a confrontation. What this tactic did, however, was to make Hutchison really pissed off with me.

Things came to a head later on that fateful day. Michael's son, Luke, began verbally abusing me out in the line-up because he thought I had "dropped in" on a young surfer we both knew. Unbeknownst to the strapping lad, our mutual friend had actually called me to go, as he couldn't catch the wave. After repeatedly trying to explain that the kid had given me the wave, I paddled over to Luke, who was screaming obscenities at the top of his lungs. He wouldn't listen to me, so, out of frustration, I swatted him in the mouth, in the way you would smack a puppy when it does the wrong thing. It was the only option I felt I had left to get him to shut up.

A little later, Michael caught up with me on the beach and began pounding me unmercifully, all the while saying how I didn't even recognise his existence and how everybody thought I was God, but now he was. I should have said something, but I couldn't get a word out. I should have tried to defend myself, but my left hand was wrapped in a waterproof bandage since I had lopped the top of my thumb off with a chainsaw the day before. He was punching me around my head, telling me to have a go, saying how I'd had this coming for a long time.

It was my worst nightmare. Michael beat on me until I stumbled and fell to the ground. I could feel the blood running down my face, saw it pooling on the sand. The amount of blood was amazing; I knew it was serious. Then he started kicking my back; the pain running through me was intense.

Beau helped me up, but I couldn't stand by myself – not very well anyhow. I was swaying, going in and out of focus, when the blows to my face started again, all in exactly the same place, one fist after another, hitting between the eye sockets and the top jaw. It was beyond any pain I have ever felt before. I had no more clarity. Then, for some reason, Michael stopped. I don't know why. He just let me go.

Beau commandeered a friend's car, and the nightmare of doctors and X-rays began. That first night the sedation was so heavy a nurse had to sit with me in the hospital to make sure I continued breathing. The scans showed multiple fractures to the front of my face. Six and a half hours of reconstructive facial surgery later (at one of the best hospitals in Sydney) and the road to recovery is well defined. With rest and love, it should be possible to put my life back together.

Thanks to the hands of a brilliant surgeon, and to the properties of titanium (which will hold the reconstruction in shape until the mashed bone and titanium knit together and become a solid form), I may one day have something that looks and feels like my old face. The surgeon says it will be a year or so before the feeling returns between my top teeth and eye sockets. The nerves were severed, so it'll take time for them to join up, or regrow, or whatever it is that nerves do.

Meanwhile, as I've been healing, I've been looking for causes and reasons for the attack. The fact that Michael was the only one surfing a long board on the fateful day was perhaps the primary trigger; however, his pent-up rage had became so intense over the years that it's hard to say exactly what caused his extreme reaction. In his defence, I have to admit that I had an attitude about long boards out at The Point – always have had. Now I realise my attitude was not healthy. It's wrong to have a prejudice about anything or anyone, and I am working on correcting it.

Four months after the incident, I am looking pretty good. Things seem back to normal, and I'm surfing every day on either short or long boards. The wounds have healed completely on the outside, but on the inside it still really hurts. The single biggest thing that has caused the most anxiety to my family and me has been the lack of support by some people we considered close friends in this small community. In this respect, it has been a good way to find out where these people are really at, but it's an ongoing, painful exercise every day.

In order not to become bitter and twisted ourselves, we have had to come to terms with seeing these people and discussing their public comments. We simply cannot smile and pretend that things are the same after reading their quotes in the media. Some of them came to us when I first returned from hospital, inquiring about my health and complaining about being misquoted on the television or in the newspapers. I know only too well about the gutter-raking sleazebag Sydney press and the extent to which they will go to invent a story.

Although the amount of love and good wishes I

received from friends in this area, Australia and all over the world was phenomenal, it's become clear to us that we will be leaving the beautiful Angourie. We will sell our holiday complex and stay away — at least until the internal wounds heal.

Some of you reading this already know and understand that I did not intend to get involved in another book project so soon. Basically, I felt like I needed to rest for a while after the extensive amount of brain drain associated with writing, publishing and marketing my autobiography, *Nat's Nat and That's That* (Nymboida Press, 1999). I figured it was time to let other people comment on the state of surfing as it develops into the new century, and I would just sit back and be an observer. That was a nice thought; however, I find it impossible, given my present situation.

Background

It's so easy for some people to say how lucky I have been throughout my life, how everything has come quite easily. I believe that is very simplistic and totally wrong. What I have achieved has come through paying attention to details and hard work, and the key to my success is that I have been very adept at turning negatives into positives.

I remember one of the first times this happened. I was 15, in serious training for the 1963 Australian Open Surfing Championships, and I cut my foot badly on a broken bottle while running down the beach behind my family's home in Collaroy, just north of Sydney. With just a few days before the contest began, I was devastated. I could have given up and pulled out, but I had been working on my surfing style for years, and the moment was at hand. I was a junior going in the seniors; I knew it was my time, and I just had to go for it.

I did not "hassle" anyone out of a wave in that contest at Bondi, nor at any time in the event. I gave other competitors waves, and they did the same for me. That was the last time I remember going in a contest and not fighting to win. No success tasted as good as that one in '63. First prize was a first-class air ticket around the world, supplied by the *Sunday Telegraph* newspaper and its owner, the late Sir Frank Packer. I knew winning was my only way out of mediocre suburban Sydney, and so I had won the contest with my foot all bandaged up and hurting like hell, but I turned that accident into a positive.

The same thing has happened again and again over the years. One particularly dramatic example of turning a negative into a positive occurred much later on, some 30 years later, in January 1994.

I was snowboarding with my family in Sun Valley, Idaho, when I hit a large patch of ice from a faulty snow gun. I flew over a cliff and collided with a pine tree on the way down, splitting my head open. The time in hospital recovering from the serious head wound was where I got into working on *Nat's Nat and That's That*. If it wasn't for the time required for convalescing, I would never have been disciplined enough to take the time to sit down and write my autobiography in longhand.

I intend to do exactly the same with this latest incident, which left me beaten to a pulp, my face still feeling like I had just been to the dentist four months after the assault. Now I have to get over my problems, turn this negative into a positive, and get on with my life. But I can't help thinking about where all this "Surf Rage" is going. Where will it end? Why is this disease running unchecked through our culture?

In retrospect, this first year of the new millennium seems like one of the worst of my life. I had attempted to get things off to a good start with a family boarding and skiing holiday in the Italian Dolomites in January. But things went rapidly downhill when my nine-year-old son was involved in a hit-and-run accident on the slopes that caused him to lose all his adult front teeth. Friends tell me I should have taken it as an omen, but I didn't. I just kept pushing, but it seemed like "bad luck" kept dogging me and my family.

A few months later, while I was in Europe again, doing promotional work for the Bic company, my wife Ti was awakened from a sound sleep at 4.30 a.m. A man was screaming abuse and kicking at the front door of our house, which adjoins the holiday units at Angourie. She ran down the hall still half-asleep, tripped on the front step, and fell, breaking her nose in three places and slicing open her forehead to the tune of ten stitches.

Apparently the guy was one of our arriving guests! He had called earlier, asking if he could check in at 9.30 a.m., which he was told was no problem. Then, for some reason, he arrived at 4.30 a.m., expecting a key to have been left out for him. He became frustrated, lost it and never did apologise, although his wife was extremely embarrassed.

Guest Rage! Such is the state of the world these days.

State of the Art
I think surfing organisations, the media, and surf-related corporations share some responsibility for the present state of affairs among surfers. I think that they – we – have fed the fire by directly or indirectly condoning violence in the surf. We've made "stars" out of some of the very surfers who commit these crimes, and they are crimes. Individually and collectively, we have all turned a blind eye to Surf Rage.

We have all known about it for a long time; we've watched it fester all over the world. However, like most things in life, it's not until it affects you or your family that you feel compelled to do something about it.

The extent of the injuries I received on 16 March at my home break of Angourie has forced me to do something, to attempt to bring serious attention to this issue. As I write these words, I am going into the eighth week of recovery, and, as I do so, I find myself talking to people all over the world about how bad the situation is at their beaches, about how something has to be done to expose this degrading violence.

In some respects the state of surfing today really saddens me, especially in those moments when I consider just how much our beloved sport has fundamentally changed in the last 40 years of its short 100-year modern history.

The changes I'm referring to are certainly not apparent on the surface, not revealed in the incredible moves being attempted by everyone from the kids to the pros every time they enter the water these days. What I'm referring to is at the very core of our surfing. These changes have crept up on us in an insidious way. We almost haven't noticed them as they have gradually become so commonplace that we don't much remember or care how it was before.

I find myself asking the same question over and over again: is surfing still the enjoyable all-encompassing experience that our forebears enjoyed and practised at every opportunity? As I've been told (and can remember), surfing was all about a fun day at the beach with your friends.

That may have been the way it was, but I sincerely fear that it will never be like that again. The pace of living has accelerated – not for everyone, but for the majority of those who surf. Whether we like it or not, we surfers are part of a culture which seems to be increasingly competitive, reflecting the frustrations of this very crowded planet on which we live.

I believe that competition has much to answer for in this change of attitude by a large portion of the surfing public. Quite often older surfers will tell you that surfing competitions back in the '60s were really cool events. I can still remember when I was a kid, contests were called "meets"; some old Hawaiians still call 'em that. They were an excuse for a really good get-together, where friends and the whole family went surfing just for fun, ate together, and if someone was lucky enough to win a trophy that was fine, but it wasn't as important as the gathering of the tribe.

By the time I was actively competing in 1964 and '65, much of this reality had already disappeared. Winning became more important than any social or cultural interaction. I remember that it was very different after that point in time.

Some people believe the development of "man-on-man" competition in the mid-'70s (where only two competitors are allowed in the water at a time) changed the feel of the contests. I remember watching the first man-on-man event at Burleigh Heads in southern Queensland, and I'm sure almost everyone saw it as a definite step forward for professional competition; it certainly made surfing contests easier to watch and understand. The rules and method of judging were more defined, and the winner was usually very clear cut.

Some people believe it was the advent of prize money that was surfing's undoing. Surfers were so hungry for cash they fought like cats and dogs for the best possible waves on which to show off their skills. Those precious few dollars back in the '70s and '80s would allow us to continue the tour to the next competition, to the next "surf fix" in the next far-off country. We would do almost anything for a pittance in the early days of professional competition.

Well, it isn't so different now. Just ask yourself, how far would you push the point to get the best wave and win the contest? Would you "snake" another competitor if you knew he was out to snake you? Would you drop in on him or her? I have committed or observed these and other acts of unsportsmanlike behaviour at almost every contest I have been around for the past 20 years. It's generally accepted by the touring "pros", even by the kids at some little monthly club contests.

Occasionally there have been fights between competitors at professional competitions over what is very loosely termed "hassling" for the best wave.

Just this year, up on the Gold Coast, Samantha Cornish and Trudy Todd were surfing in the semifinals of the Quiksilver/Roxy contest and almost came to blows on the beach. The utter amazement on the faces of a thousand spectators as they watched Trudy grab Sam in a headlock and ram her head into the sand was very telling. Apparently Sam had been "hassling" Trudy by paddling around her to get at a wave that Trudy intended to ride, but does that warrant such violence?

Ask anyone who followed the ASP men's tour back in 1990 about the time Damien Hardman "snaked" Tom Carroll in the final of the Coke Classic at Narrabeen. I was disgusted by Dooma's action when he turned around in the whitewater while paddling out and stood up on the inside of the same wave, scoring a technical interference on Carroll. He recently defended his action by saying that he really needed the money for a house payment. I believe Damien's credibility seriously suffered that day, and surfing was morally (if not mortally) wounded.

What the pros do and how they behave is a mirror of what happens in a normal surf scene. The technical interference rule came out of the "drop in" rule, which states that a surfer up and riding has the right of way and should not be dropped in on by another surfer. This is one of the fundamental unwritten laws of surfing.

Such provocative incidents in professional surfing contests are only the tip of the iceberg, and they're not unique to surfing. It's the same in all sports these days, from tennis players smashing rackets on the court to soccer games where loyal fans get into punch-ups in support of their teams.

Violence is everywhere.

The problem in surfing, as I see it, is that no-one – from the pros to everyday surfers – realises that there is no difference between competition and normal every-day surfing. Every surfer in a contest knows the rules; it doesn't matter what the head judge sees or doesn't see, it's a matter of what is right and wrong – by the unwritten rules. Everyone knows what is right. It's even more clear-cut in everyday surfing – if you don't give respect, you won't get it. That's the bottom line.

I spoke with my 25-year-old son about these unwrit-ten rules, and he had some pretty definite thoughts. Having just returned from teaching surfing to begin-ners in Japan, Beau felt that some sort of a ranking for each particular break would really help the situation. Then you would avoid the chaos of 30 beginners in the line-up, surfing alongside competent surfers.

Such changes would be just about impossible to implement at this point in the game, but basic rules (like using the rip to paddle out, staying in the white water as long as necessary, and paying particular atten-tion not to be caught in the line of the surfer riding the wave) are, well, basic.

These are the laws that everyone, from experts to beginners, must observe, and naturally, the more experienced you become the more you learn to avoid potential problem situations.

A classic that I see quite regularly is when a broken wave is approaching or breaks on top of a beginner, and they " bail out", slipping off the board and letting the leash take care of it. They have no idea where they are in the impact zone, how far the leash will stretch, or whether or not the loose board – which is potentially a lethal weapon – will strike another surfer.

Both Beau and I believe that the surfer waiting the longest should have the right of way; however, should he or she paddle and miss the wave, then they should lose that priority and go back to the end of the queue. This suggestion dovetails with the unwritten rule that the surfer closest to the peak, or the first to be on his or her feet, has priority. It's all about communication; you have to let the other people know if you're going for a wave and, if it's a peak, which way you intend to go.

Who is to Blame?
Everyone seems to have an opinion on when and why surfing fundamentally changed, but one thing is for certain: Surf Rage is not only thriving on the beaches where I live on the north coast of New South Wales in Australia, it is burning like a bushfire everywhere in the world. It has become so bad in some areas of the United States that police patrol the line-ups on jet skis during the summer months.

Does this mean violence is as out of control on the beaches as it is on some big-city streets, and that a strong police presence is necessary to defuse potentially volatile situations?

I hope not.

Obviously, a greater concentration of people

means potentially more aggression. The island of Oahu in Hawaii has a high incidence of Surf Rage due to a large (and growing) surfing population and, therefore, greater competition for the waves. With so many surfing tourists coming to Hawaii every year in search of their perfect wave, competition is fierce. The harsh reality is that the locals are threatened by outsiders continually cutting into their already limited wave supply.

To put the shoe on the other foot, however, it's hard for the tourist to give respect when he or she still hasn't caught a single one of those big Hawaiian barrels that he or she has spent six months scrimping and saving for. After all that time working away, seeing the perfect wave in the mind's eye, you just have to go for that big Pipeline tube, even if it does mean dropping in on some other unfortunate surfer.

The size of the surfing population of a country does not necessarily reflect the attitude of the surfers, however. Brazil has a relatively small number of surfers compared with the United States, yet travelling Brazilian wave riders have a reputation for being the most aggressive of any nation. An informal assessment finds that in Indonesia, Australia, and Hawaii they have been in more surf-related fights than surfers of any other nationality.

In Europe, the popularity of surfing has exploded. One barometer, Quiksilver's sales of surf-related products, rocketed to $US450 million in 1999. It's just a little over 30 years since Wayne Lynch, Ted Spencer and I were among the first to wander over the sand dunes at Hossegor, and now every summer thousands of surfers from all over Europe visit those perfect beach breaks. Unfortunately, in recent years, Surf Rage is boiling away at Hossegor and at every other hot French surf break, too. Perhaps it's the fiery European blood that gets these surfers into fights, with locals ganging up on tourists, locals against locals. It's crazy.

I've even seen fights break out in the line-up in the South Pacific paradise of Tahiti, and I've witnessed other brutal acts at Tavarua on Fiji. It can happen wherever a quality wave is breaking, anywhere there is more than a single group of friends is out in the surf.

I wonder what it will take for the majority of surfers to realise that Surf Rage goes against everything that surfing is. Being aggressive and hogging all the waves is not going to get you more satisfaction. When you paddle out, you should leave your problems on the beach; don't bring your frustrations from work or home out into the surf with you.

If you paddle out with the right attitude, the ocean will cleanse you. It's like being a little boy or girl again; it can be like going home to your mother – letting her rock you in her arms. It's okay, you can relax, your Mother Ocean can soothe the pain. She can help you work it out if you give her a chance.

I have recently become acquainted with this verse, entitled "Love Letter to the Ocean" from the *Eagles Wings* newsletter by Astron (1991). It seems to fit.

I have been away from you for
So long
Yet each time I return
You accept me.

And once again you allow me to drown
In your fathomless love.
I change so much.

I am never the same person
That you knew when last we
Were together.

And you are always there.

And I will always know that.

The security I feel from you,
The love and acceptance,
Can never be given by a person
In such unequalled, selfless honesty,
As it can by you.

Each time we reunite
I feel you before I can hear you,
Before I can see you.

The growing urgency surges
Over my senses,
One at a time, mounting to a wave
That floods me with emotion.

When, finally, you embrace me:
An embrace that washes and cleanses
All my hurts and sorrows of the past
And makes me whole again.

I think this writing reflects the same mind-set as our forefathers, who went to the surf after dealing with their everyday problems – real problems like world wars, feeding their families during the Depression, and all the other small and earth-shattering events that happened way back before there was any substantial number of surfers.

Those pioneers made it possible for us to ride waves like we do now; we must never forget the debt that we owe them and the respect we should show to each other, and to ourselves.

It's all about attitude, or mind set.

I have already given you some understanding of how my attitude developed over the past 40 years of surfing. I'm not proud of everything I have done, that's for sure. But I believe that what happened to me in my formative years was pretty typical of lots of us Baby Boomers, who didn't fight in any wars, grew up with the Beatles and experienced sexual freedom.

In retrospect, perhaps we had it too easy.

We have to ask ourselves, how can we get over our prejudices? Maybe it's boogie-boarders we dislike, or knee-boarders or even women boogie-boarders. What is it that flips us out? Goat boats (surf skis) wasting waves? Just the crowds? Well, the crowds aren't going away, and it's certain that in the future there will be more of everything, except waves. Just more and more people trying to ride the same number of waves, since wave pools and artificial reefs (even if fully developed) won't satisfy the world's wave hunger, won't quench Surf Rage.

The way out of Surf Rage is a tough one. We have to learn to be more tolerant. We have to put it all in perspective. This is for real. It is not a dress rehearsal.

As Krishnamurti said, "inner revolution is more effective than social revolution". Surfers, including myself, have frequently expressed concerns on a number of social and political issues, but we have been slow to look at our own attitudes and behaviour.

This can change.

MAINLINING

(No longer a hip youth sport, surfing is now as embedded in the national psyche as football and tennis.)

Derek Rielly

Surfers? We're a mob of greedy, adrenalin-fuelled colonials participating in an unbelievably frustrating activity that drags out our worst instincts. And, as for the existence of a surfing brotherhood, that disappeared long ago in any mass sense – around the same time the industry and competition bodies completed their successful lunge for mainstream – and world-wide – acceptance, and overcrowding in the surf became endemic.

Increasingly, surfers are losing it.

Fists are thrown, knives are brandished, out-of-towners are ganged up on, cars are vandalised and boards are speared at heads.

Why?

The 1972 movie "Morning of the Earth" gave us a cultural snapshot of Australian surfing during that distant hippie epoch. One five-minute section depicted a 22-year-old surfer, David "Baddy" Treloar, building a surfboard in his backyard in his boardshorts, then running down to his local point to test his creation, all to the G Wayne Thomas song "Gentle Ben".

Just over a quarter of a century later and Baddy's mate Nat Young has his face reduced to mash on the same point and the man responsible has such a hold on the lineup Baddy refuses to surf while he's in the water.

At Burleigh Heads, on Queensland's Gold Coast, surfers are punched for offences such as surfing behind a local, attempting to catch a wave, accidentally getting in the way, falling off or for riding a longboard.

Anyone foolish enough to wear colourful attire is branded as having aggressively homosexual tendencies.

In Bali, foreign surfers are regularly ordered in from the surf by the Black Shorts, a gang of local surfers who've modelled themselves after the infamous Hawaiian surfing club, the Hui 'O He'e Nalu, or are set upon by two or three when they argue the point.

Rocks are thrown at surfers and their cars vandalised in the Canary Islands. Fuck up in Brazil and you'll get a close look at the mechanics of jujitsu. Local surfers in Mauritius are infamous for their short tempers and love of shivs. On the North Shore of Oahu – the very seat of surf thuggery – enthusiasts of violent activity can switch off Ultimate Wrestling on cable, sit themselves down on a patch of sand overlooking Rocky Point and watch as tempers fray and fists become the only rule.

And, unbelievably, at Munich's Eisbach, rocks are thrown at unfamiliar photographers if they shoot photos of Bavaria's premier wave, encouraging a mass invasion of surfers if the photos head outside Germany.

There has always been violence in surfing. It is atavistic, difficult to excel at, and adrenalin spurts through our bodies at even the sight of a good wave. Psychologists refer to the Expert Rule, which says that after ten years of hard, deliberate practice, you'll become an expert at any activity, whether it's music, dance or chess.

Surfing violates the rule.

Mastery is always out of our grasp as we struggle daily to deal with the moving, unpredictable elements. Where a snowboarder can practise the same aerial manoeuvre a hundred times in a day – a chairlift providing rest between runs – the surfer might only find a willing section once or twice per surf.

And after each wave he has to use all that shoulder

strength and heart power to make it back to the line-up for the chance, hopefully, of replicating the ride. Kelly Slater has been surfing for twenty-five of his twenty-nine years and he says he is further away from mastery than ever.

Alpha males dominate surf spots and locals are, and have always been, mostly reactionary hillbillies. And the rules of surfing are complex and fluid. They change to suit the amount of time a surfer has spent at a surf spot, and how well he surfs, thus confusing the cockles out of the beginner and putting them in a position they have no idea how to get out of and causing flashes of tempers from surfers who expect order at their break.

But it has gotten worse.

There has been a paradigm shift in the surfing culture, from one fiercely anti-establishment and pro-drugs that regarded the line-up as an escape from the bullshit of the world to one that is increasingly aggressive, conservative and competition-driven yet, paradoxically, constantly working to attract more participants.

The number of surfers has increased, hierarchies at surf spots are gradually being broken down as easy-to-ride vehicles, such as the modern long board and boogie board, change the playing field, enabling novices to compete with surfers who've spent thirty years in the ocean.

Surfing isn't about kids any more. The lifestyle includes both sexes and every age and occupation. Lounge singers, entrepreneurs, lawyers, actors, football players, men in their seventies, mothers, grandmothers, lovers, fighters, all are represented. If you're a long-time surfer, ask yourself this: would you become a surfer if you were a kid in 2000?

I wouldn't – nor would any of the friends I asked in a totally-unscientific snap poll.

Without the cool, the edginess and the thrill of clinging to a counter-culture there's nothing to keep you connected with the activity long enough to experience its deeper, ultimately-satisfying joys. Skating and snowboarding are the hip sports at the start of this century.

How easy it is to become surfer now.

Like to learn? Call a surf school, there's one operating at a variety of convenient times and at a beach nearby. Mum and Dad'll be pleased you've decided to join such a healthy band of athletes, most apparently anti-drugs. And doesn't that stocky Italian chap, Mark Occhilupo, make a million dollars a year?

A surfboard? The rebirth of the old Malibu has made standing up a cinch, and there's definitely no shortage of craftsmen delighted with the demand for the archaic craft charging amounts manufacturers of high-performance shortboards can only dream of. And to remove any form of danger from the learning process you can even buy giant rubber boards. If that sounds too hard, buy a bodyboard. Does anybody out there under thirty recall what a fringe culture surfing once was? How parents would stand terrified on the front verandah as their 16-year-old daughter disappeared into the cabin of a Holden HG panel van with surfboards tied to the roof? How police would target any surfer-laden Kombi van for drug searches? Or the fear beachside takeaway owners had of surfers and the suburban petrol heads suddenly erupting into gang warfare on their quiet little retail stretch?

To be a surfie meant you were not only a connoisseur of those fabulous bands of energy that manifest their physical presence via waves but a drug enthusiast. And it was all lovingly documented by that once counter-culture magazine, *Tracks*, then a cheap newspaper-stock tabloid produced out of Whale Beach on Sydney's northern beaches. The magazine's long running cartoon, Captain Goodvibes, featured a mull-smoking, sexually-voracious pig – an apt metaphor for surfers.

That *Tracks* is now a high-quality, formulaic glossy owned by British publishing giants EMAP and designed in the likeness of the company's flagship *FHM* is a striking comment on where the Australian surfing culture is today.

Surf shops were once as exclusive as Masonic lodges. Typically, they were in difficult-to-find locations, though close to the beach. In one small room there would be crammed upwards of thirty surfboards of differing dimensions. The remaining space was consumed by perhaps one rack of what appeared to be homemade t-shirts, four or so pairs of boardshorts in wildly different sizes, and, in the glass cabinet beneath the ancient handle-operated cash register, Bolle and Vuarnet sunglasses, a leg rope and a few blocks of wax. The man behind the counter – often the shaper who'd created the boards that crowded the shop – would eye you with suspicion and would mutter something under his breath to the ever-present sponsored grommet, a young surfer loaded with talent and attitude. You'd feel the scorch of embarrassment as you moved between the boards, rubbing the rails inexpertly and trying to see the subtle design touches that made each surfboard perform so differently. Other surfers would come in, sometimes the best surfers from the beach, and deride you and your attempt to enter the scene, with no attempt to conceal their antipathy. Yet, these young men, strong and brown, all it seemed at the time with perfectly honey-blond curly hair, with the quick humour and dazzling arrogance, only made surfing more appealing.

What a contrast to today's surf emporiums where spunky chicklings with the dazzling smiles – most of whom would soil their cottontails if confronted by the medium after which their boutique is named – are at the ready to help you sort through the maze of surf fashion.

Surfboards have all but disappeared from most surf shops, the profit margin too slim to be viable for the amount of space they take up. For good or bad, surfing has become more accessible, and even if you don't buy the shift in the culture as the primary reason, the increased numbers suggest that even by averages, fighting and tension have to be on the increase.

A 1999 Australian Sports Commission-funded survey found that 13 per cent of the Australian population claimed to surf, up from a steady 11 per cent throughout the nineties.

Unless the respondents are bullshitting, that's nearly two-and-a-half million Australians who surf.

Why do we get the shits in the line-up? Blame a combination of territoriality, the human instinct to protect what is perceived to be ours, testosterone (surfing being virtually entirely male) and adrenalin.

Fights rarely happen while surfers are waiting for waves. It is when the adrenalin starts to flow, during a paddle battle or a drop in, that frustration spills over and we exhibit extreme behaviour.

If you're surfing eight-foot Pipe, where one mistake can mean serious injury, and another surfer fades you into the bowl, how are you going to react? Chances are you'll behave differently than if someone took your car space at the local supermarket. Have you noticed that Surf Rage incidents occur exclusively between an established local and an outsider or two locals on the same rung in the pecking order? A grommet won't attack an elder, nor will two outsiders be driven to sufficient frenzy to pummel each other. This shows us that the violence is territorial, not random. Like dogs, we mark off and protect what we perceive to be ours. Go to a beach or park and see how timid a new dog to the area is until he's marked off with urine – territorial pissing – his property. Similarly, watch a surfer new to a surf spot and, initially, he'll be low-key until he marks off his own piece. Before long he too begins to growl at interlopers and outsiders.

When I took up a job at *Australia's Surfing Life* magazine a decade ago and began surfing Burleigh Heads every day I began a lengthy due-paying exercise from one of the area's most vocal locals. The wave itself is a fantastic, interesting creature. From Sharkies in front of the headland through the Cove, the Point and Rockbreak it's a blend of difficult, heavy barrels (Sharkies), big take-offs (Cove) and dreamy speed runs (Point).

The aforementioned local showed a remarkable determination not to allow any sort of civil contact, despite my fairly low-key approach and friendships with various other locals. His name? Dwayne Harris. You might have heard of him. Thirty-eight years old. Lived at Burleigh since 1972 though his grandparents have been in Burleigh since the '30s, younger brother of Glenn (45) and Peter (43, and the 1980 Stubbies winner), strong naturalfooter, sits right on the Point during a swell and takes any wave he wants pretty much whether or not you, I, or anyone else is on it.

Seven years ago, coincidentally around the time I started surfing the place every day, *ASL* published a smart-arse story entitled "Can Burleigh Learn to Love?"

It was part of a feature documenting dysfunctional surf spots around the globe and jabbed the piss-take stick at a few of Burleigh's long-time locals. One excerpt reads: "Angry locals like Dwayne and Peter Harris and tubby goofyfooter Nick Heath seem to spend more time swearing at tourists than riding waves

... Dwayne Harris declined to be interviewed for this piece, declaring flatly: 'I don't believe in localism. I just go out there and take any wave.' When *ASL* suggested it might be a good opportunity for him to inform visiting surfers how to behave themselves, he was unmoved. 'You can't tell 'em. They're all mindless.'"

Ignoring the fact that I had no part in writing the piece and that my heterosexuality would've been without question had he asked any of the local women who'd suffered my invading member, Dwayne began a relentless outing campaign. Every decent swell whenever I ran back up the headland to the Cove's jump-off rocks he'd be there in the shed yelling: "Faggot! Faggot! Faggot!" Went on for years. It was so ongoing, so unabated that I felt like I was in some one-sided war. Never before had I encountered such institutionalised localism, hints of it in Margaret River and in north-west WA, sure, and obviously in Hawaii, but never on such a grand scale in Australia.

I didn't have a problem with the guy, and his being sheriff in the water did slow down the crowds. And the more time I put into Burleigh the more I felt a sense of proprietorship about it. I thought it was a bit weird how he was hammering the homo point, but that's what you get around these parts. I even managed a little admiration for Dwayne when I beached a wave near the pool on a warm Sunday afternoon and he was there on the beach helping beginners get their first taste of the ocean. Smiling. Encouraging. I eventually confronted Dwayne about the faggot thing at Rabbit Bartholomew and Tim Baker's *Busting Down the Door* book launch at the Snapper surf club and asked him what was up.

He visibly cringed when I approached and said something like: "It's nothing personal. It's just that *ASL* should do more stuff on the Burleigh groms". Fair enough. I told him it was kind of hard to do anything on the Burleigh kids when they're giggling behind him while he mounts a vocal campaign about my aggressive homosexuality. So we wound up, I thought, on friendly terms. I said g'day when I saw him checking the surf and riding around on his mountain bike. He hated it, though, and this unconditional friendliness seemed to seriously freak him out. And, every swell without fail, he was dropping in, doing reos in my face and launching into the faggot tirade as I ran back around the point. Then, at a little gig *ASL* put on during the Billabong Pro, he came straight up to me, thanked me for letting him and the Burleigh boys come in and get stuck into the free piss and so I let it all out again, the whole faggot thing.

He told me it's a due-paying thing, that Gordo (Channel 7 cameraman and a bit of a legend around the Gold Coast) had had to put up with it for ten years and that we were actually sort of mates. I gave a speech thanking the Burleigh guys, and we wound up dancing with a bunch of pissed pro surfer girls on the dance floor, Dwayne coming the closest I've ever seen to happiness.

We bought each other (and the rest of the Burleigh guys) drinks when the tab finished, raved about surfing, Brad Jeffrie's brilliant backhand tuberiding, the grommets, old legends and other stuff for hours. Champion bloke. Next swell comes and, fuck, he's still there calling me a faggot.

So what do you do? If you're a journalist, you conduct an interview. Get it in the open and smash it like a rotten egg. The local and the man he hates. Together at last. A couple of mates later said we looked like a couple of world leaders involved in a rigorous peace talks, seated at a table, microcassette upright between us, our figures silhouetted in the

Burleigh shed. The interview makes an interesting read, an insight into the mind of the archetypal local:

DR: Do you feel like you play a certain role here?

Dwayne: I'd like to hope I'm a role model for young guys around here.

DR: What do you like to teach the kids?

Dwayne: Respect's the first thing they should learn. A lot of kids these days don't have a lot of respect for elder people, whether it be surfers or elder people. I got brought up to respect elder people. If there was more respect in the water there wouldn't be as much hassles going on. It's not that the boys are aggro, we're just trying to keep it respectful. I've got respect for guys who've surfed here longer than me. I don't drop in on them. I think it should filter down through all the people.

DR: What's the construction of the hierarchy out at Burleigh, like which guys won't you drop in on?

Dwayne: Sorta filters down from Doris (Eltherington), I think. There's a few of the old crew I don't drop in on. It's hard, though. I've got a bad surf addiction. It's hard not to. When you're sitting out there for 10, 15 minutes and you don't get any waves and you see all these other people getting waves you sorta go, well, I deserve one of those. It's not being a mongrel or an arsehole or anything, it's just being wave hungry. That's all it is. I like a lot of waves.

DR: It's a fine line between a respectful order in the lineup and one that's overtly violent. Burleigh's about the only point left on the Gold Coast with any sort of control, but at what cost?

Dwayne: Well, you know, it happens. Like, at Kirra there's locals but they don't police it any more. It could be worse out here. Burleigh'd be a lot worse if the locals weren't here. But compared to the old days it's nothing. It was a lot heavier back then. There's no violence compared to what it was because you get sued now.

DR: What was it like in the '70s and '80s?

Dwayne: It was like the wild west when I was growing up here. They didn't argue in them days. They were heavy boys. They just paddled over and punched 'em out and sent 'em in.

DR: Do you feel yourself getting tense in the water?

Dwayne: I do. Yeah, I get tense. If it's over four foot I try and sort it out in the water, if it's under four foot I just go in. I don't like getting angry in the water anymore. I do get angry but I don't like it. I'll go in and come back out when I've settled down. But a few guys get angry and get into fights, but you need that, you need that out there. After you see a good bit of biffo go down, the lineup clears itself a bit. It does it good. It really needs it some days. You need a fight to sort it out. It happens down D-Bah too. You surf D-Bah and there's guys like Bruce Lee and they keep it policed ...

DR: But it's not as intense as Burleigh.

Dwayne: Nah, nothing's like here. Except Hawaii.

DR: So Burleigh's heaps mellower now?

Dwayne: You've got a few crew that get angry, but I reckon it's much mellower. Except the crowds are more ... there's just more idiots.

DR: Do you realise when you're starting to lose it?

Dwayne: I start surfing really bad. Don't get any waves. You get shitty and you paddle for waves and you miss 'em and you get even angrier. I go in now. I'd rather go home, mellow out, come back when, hopefully, I'm a bit mellower. Surfing's a release. A lot of people don't have releases and that's why you have violence. Because they don't have a release, they're locked in some town in Ipswich or in the middle of nowhere and they've got no release for their energy and they go out and kill or rob. That's how they get rid of their excess energy.

DR: Do you feel a sense of ownership about the place?

Dwayne: Nuh, nah. Not ownership, more a sense of being part of it. Not owning it or caretaking it, just being part of it. Part of the headland, part of the whole spirit. I haven't got a career, I've got no mortgage, I could do this the rest of my life.

DR: When it gets ugly out here, do you think, fuck it, I'm in?

Dwayne: Oh yeah, I go in when it gets really ugly. I don't like it when it gets the full aggro. It takes the fun out of it. That's not what surfing's meant to be. We've got to realise we're all part of the same tribe. All the ones that don't go in the water they're the ones who're out to get us, aren't they? But the aggro does upset me. But it depends on the mood. Sometimes you don't mind it.

DR: What about our strange relationship?

Dwayne: Well, there was that article plus I'd like to see more done on the young guys around here. That's the only reason I used to get upset because you were based here and you didn't do a lot on the Burleigh crew … (pause). I don't know what it was, Derek. I think I just get like that a bit with people.

DR: How does the concept of dues paying work with you?

Dwayne: It's time and respect. Getting to know a few crew. Surfing the place all the time. Some years you don't get much swell and you have to surf shit out here all year and you get a swell and you've got all these blow-ins from other places coming to take your waves. It's selfish but when you've been waiting here all year, when it comes, you want to get your share of waves because you've put up with all the shit.

DR: How do you know when you've paid your dues?

Dwayne: When the boys start leaving you alone. It took me years. The first hassle I ever had out here was with Doris. I got in his way or something and he held my head under water. In those days there was respect because we had to hang down the end section. We weren't allowed out the point.

DR: What'd happen if you paddled out at the point?

Dwayne: They'd order you back or hold your head under water or push you over the falls on a big one.

DR: Have you travelled outside Burleigh much?

Dwayne: Nah, I've been to Hawaii once and New Zealand a couple of times and that's about it. Been to, you know, down to Victoria and Sydney. Never been able to afford it much.

DR: Have you learnt how to respect?

Dwayne: Oh yeah, mate, fuckin' oath. Wherever I go I respect the locals. I'll sit on the outside and wait my turn. That's what it's all about. That's all they want. That's all the local crew out here want. To get waves they wanna get without hassling 'em.

DR There's the odd loose cannon, though.

Dwayne: Oh yeah, there's a few. Always has been around Burleigh though.

DR: What about us now, I reckon I've paid a fair few dues, are we cool?

Dwayne: Yeah, that's (laughing) ... we're cool.

DR: So when I'm running around the point you won't be calling me a faggot?

Dwayne: Nah, I won't. Dunno about the other cunts. But it won't be me yelling out.

Another beautiful example of surf territorialism in action is in the Mentawai Islands, a leisurely overnight boat ride from the coastal city of Padang in Sumatra.

Ten years ago, the area was unsurfed. An article in *Australia's Surfing Life* revealed a little of the magic of the area, further media trips followed and, now, the islands play host to around twenty charter boats during the season.

It's in these situations that the surfing truism, "a local is someone who's been there a day longer than you", comes into play. At the name breaks, such as Lance's Rights and Macaroni's, if a boat has been there for one day or even an hour longer than another boat, its passengers will automatically assume locals' rights to the break, groaning with displeasure as the boat moves into the bay and even dropping in and exchanging verbal blows with the new crew, having already marked out their territory.

If two boats arrive at the same time, however, a mood of cooperation tends to envelop both vessels. It is decided between skippers who'll surf first and a hierarchy is developed, much the same as the hierarchy between locals at a break.

Martin Daly, 43, has been surfing and chartering his boat for ten years, and was the skipper responsible for bringing the Mentawais to the world.

He sees this imported territorialism in action every day, but says out there in the Mentawais surfers have a chance to bring about change. "I have a theory, and I'm going to spout it," he told me and a few mates once, holding court at the stern of the *Golden Big Arrow* anchored overlooking Macaroni's.

Sensing a decent speech, I had grabbed my tape player and punched Record.

He continued: "Surfing today seems to be about all the wrong emotions – selfishness, greed, deceit – like when you go out in the surf and you snake another guy. To get waves at Burleigh or Kirra you need to be a complete and utter bad person to get waves. You've got to snake, you've got to drop in. All the worst human emotions. What we're privileged to see out here, what we can do, is here out in the water you can have all the better emotions, which are giving and consideration. We can go out and take turns. It's a luxury, a huge luxury to be out the back and you see a perfect wave and how good do you feel when a really good set wave comes through and it's your turn, everybody's taking turns, and you go, 'Hey mate, why don't you go?' And the guy turns around and says, 'You're kidding, aren't you?' But you say, 'It's your wave, mate, Go!'

"And that's giving. How good does that feel as opposed to snaking and taking waves off people, fading people, dropping in, being ugly. You can go out and take turns. It's impossible when it's really crowded but there are times when you can do it. And out here where there's a couple of boatloads of guys and though everybody's bristling about how they wanna fuck the other guy, you can go, 'We'll all wait a couple of hours before we paddle out so the guys on the other boat can get some waves. When they've had waves we'll paddle out and they can paddle in. We'll take turns.' How can we turn a bad situation into a good one? We turn it around and everybody relaxes. Gone is all the greed and the aggro and all the stupidity.

"What's the one thing usually missing? Communication. Hoot for a guy who gets a good barrel even if you don't know him. How good do you feel? This is the worst place [Martin waves a hand over the lineup]. Out here, with its small takeoff zone, it can really test the theory and the emotions of greed and selfishness. You can turn around and go, 'Fuck you, you cunt, for paddling inside me!' What works for me, and it works, is to say, 'Hey, mate, we're in the middle of nowhere and you just paddled inside everybody, what makes you think that you deserve the next set wave?' They want to get aggressive and I've had guys want to fight me but I say, 'We can fester and have everybody paddling inside each other for waves. But if we're cool everyone gets a turn for a really good one and everyone has that really great experience.' So even average surfers get good waves. Some surfers have more ability but every guy wants that wave as much as anybody else.

"Just because someone has more ability doesn't mean the other guys shouldn't get good waves. I love it when everybody moves, the pack moves, when the guy with priority starts paddling for a wave then turns around and watches you go down the line, watching for the big move and he paddles back out grinning and everyone's going, 'Yeeeaaaaah!'

"The ultimate test is when a guy on his backhand, with priority, is on the shoulder. He knows he can only make the wave from there. And he's not confident of making it from where the goofies are taking off. And everyone pulls back and gives him that wave. It humanises surfing and brings out the good things in surfing as opposed to all toe selfishness, all the bitterness, all the hate. Suddenly everybody's fucking happy instead of being unhappy and aggro. It's a luxury we can afford."

Wow, groovy, but he's right.

When I first started writing this chapter, I theorised aloud to a psychologist mate that this instinctual tendency toward violence comes from our surfing roots in Polynesia. After all, the Hawaiians, Maoris and Tahitians must be carrying some ferocious warrior genes.

Dr Paul "Hair Bear" Chandler, a surfer and in-demand psychologist from Maroubra who spends six months each year travelling (delivering lectures at universities from Sweden to South America, and surfing his brains out on the down days, particularly in his beloved South America), thought about it for a week, stuck his head in a few books at the University of New South Wales where he keeps an office, and came back with a response way out of left field.

Bear believes instances of rage have grown not from Polynesian cultures but out of distorted western values. Turns out, says Bear, that traditional Polynesian culture valued the ability to give rather than own as the measure of wealth.

For instance, a man who gave away ten pigs was regarded more than the man who owned ten pigs. Fences only existed to keep animals in, not to show boundaries. Land wasn't owned but was farmed by nomadic groups and the concepts of ownership and exclusivity of land use were foreign.

Yet Australians and Americans have always been proud that they are among the most fervent home owners in the world.

In the western cultures your social worth is largely determined by your accumulation of wealth.

A necessary outcome of this is that boundary lines are drawn, including in the ocean. Under western influence, surf spots have become another possession.

Just look at the island of Tavarua in Fiji.

A group of Americans built a resort then claimed exclusive surfing rights to a reef just off the island and another a fifteen-minute boat ride away. Money was paid to local tribes to enforce this self-created law and surfers from resorts on other islands daring to ride the reefs were told to leave or, worse, became victims of violence.

Similarly in the Maldives, the proprietor of Tari Village, Tony Hussein Hinde, claims "exclusive access" to Pasta Point, a lefthander that breaks in front of his resort. And what happens when surfing is introduced to a country, say the Solomons, Indonesia, Fiji or Samoa: how do the locals react?

It's a five-part process, Bear and I agree, beginning with admiration, then progressing through a mutual sharing of waves, a feeling that they're being hard done by, resentment and territorial behaviour.

Interestingly, Nick Carroll, surfing's most enduring commentator, reckons there could be a sixth part to the process, *reconciliation*, and points to Tahiti as an example.

When the surfers from outside started arriving, Tahitian surfers welcomed them to their breaks, gave them waves and even offered dinner invitations. Then followed an influx of Hawaiians and their western-influenced notions of ownership and iron-fisted localism.

The South Pacific Brotherhood was formed between Tahitians and Hawaiians, and a North Shore style of policing of surf spots began making Tahiti an unpleasant destination for anyone not connected to the SPB.

How is it now?

Actually, it's not that far removed from the days of yore and locals, even on notorious islands such as Huahine, offer handshakes and waves (just don't take any photos, okay?).

Still, surfers who went to Bali in the seventies and even the eighties recall smiling locals encouraging them to share the waves.

Now there are days when you don't even want to get near the water.

What does Surf Rage feel like?

Imagine driving through city traffic on a bad day, the equivalent of surfing crowded Burleigh or Bondi. In traffic, you are constantly forced to brake or change lanes as cars pull out in front of you from merging lanes or race you to the traffic lights. Accidents are only avoided through your vigilance and goodwill. You clench the steering wheel tight, your muscles tense and, though it is entirely inappropriate, violence feels like the only response.

In the surf you are forced to miss sections, pull back

on waves or blow tubes to avoid collisions.

No-one likes to be treated unfairly, and a surfer's reaction, just like the car driver's in a road rage scenario, to illegal line jumping and to those who flout the laws can go a lot further than a measured verbal attack.

At Burleigh Heads one memorable morning last year three surfers on three consecutive waves were pitched on the take off on top of me. I'd untangle one shrieking rider only to have another come falling out of the sky.

I held my temper, just.

I've seen a Burleigh local drop in on a visiting surfer, veer threateningly toward him, collide, then surface throwing punches at the stunned bloke. Karma had its cosmic way in this situation, however. The visitor turned out to be a gun bluer and shut his assailant down with a highly polished combination of punches and elbows to the head.

But like most surfers of mildly unstable temperament, I've cracked. Some years ago I attempted to connect the nose of my surfboard with the brain of a flatmate who'd earlier dropped in on me. Before the surf I'd found my girlfriend on the receiving end of an enthusiastic rutting from what appeared to be an extraordinarily well-built man of African origin. Her barely human grunts of pleasure tore my heart out and I stumbled back from the door without them seeing and drove home an emotional mess.

A surf was in order and, with two flatmates, I paddled across a river to a favourite surf spot. The clean four-foot tubes under the sort of hot blue sky Queensland's built a tourism industry on seemed the perfect balm to soothe my twitching emotions. A wave wedged, I paddled into it, looked down the line at its ribbed curves, smiled, stood up and missed the section as my flatmate burned the fuck out of me.

My one escape from all the bullshit of the morning had been invaded by greed and theft.

Next wave. He's on the inside, I slip off my board and fire it head high as he passes. I miss, but the heaviness of the manouevre freaked even me out. A more acutely aimed shot and the consequences could've gone way beyond a sore head or cut face. It was a primitive and clumsy overreaction. But even now, as I write, I can feel the fury of having the sweetness of this surf made bitter by just one surfer.

Similarly, years later at Duranbah on the Queensland border I was on the verge of losing it at a cowering bodyboarder, barely thirteen at my estimation. I held a swatch of his long hair in my fist and screamed in frustration at his ignorance of the hierarchy. He had dropped in and ruined what was, on this day, an extremely rare barrel. I'd observed the code, waited my turn, hooted others and was shut down by an uncaring little shit.

As I railed and clutched, his eyes bulged with, at first, fear, then confusion as I snapped back to reality, realised the ridiculousness of the scenario, and apologised over and over to him.

Some days I feel like a sheriff out there, marshalling beginners into safer parts of the reef or beach, instructing kids how to paddle, barking at beginner longboarders to go in if they can't control their dangerous craft and pointing out to others the importance of splitting a peak rather than automatically, greedily, gobbling up the best direction.

Despite all that, is Surf Rage actually a bit of a media beat up?

In a way, yes.

All over Australia, all over the world, millions of surfers coexist for the most part peacefully.

Bashings of the savagery Nat suffered are extremely

rare and it is only the overblown response of tabloid journalism, in print and television, that makes the situation appear so dire. Yet the line-ups are becoming increasingly tense and are being drawn tauter with the addition of each new surfer.

Government regulation won't work: neither is it desirable. The surf should always remain free of laws and the money-grabbing and overreaction of litigation.

The question is, will more surfers resort to fists and knives as crowds swell or will we develop mechanisms to deal with our frustration?

This book aims to corral it all into some sort of perspective – the writer of each chapter was given a loose brief and told to let all his prejudices and opinions spill onto the page, thus giving us a unique cultural snapshot of surfing – and to offer tips on how to recognise and avoid the filth and fury of Surf Rage.

After all, even with all the bullshit, surfing's still the coolest way to exercise body and soul.

DEFENDING THE FAITH

A brief history of the Secret Spot

Nick Carroll

Nick Carroll is 41 years old and is one of the world's most accomplished surf writers and journalists. He had a successful competitive surfing career, winning two Australian national titles and competing at the top pro level in Australia, Europe, Japan, Hawaii and the US, before turning his hand to journalism. He edited Australia's TRACKS magazine from 1983 to 1986, and was editor-in-chief of the SURFING magazine group in California from 1991 to 1997. He has written on surfing and other subjects for a wide range of publications, including the SYDNEY MORNING HERALD, THE AUSTRALIAN, ROLLING STONE, the NY VILLAGE VOICE, PLAYBOY, SURFER, and numerous others, and has published several books.

I have a Secret Spot. This Secret Spot is in a suburban coastal area, in plain view of anyone who cares to look. It breaks in very specific conditions, however, and in the past twenty years I have surfed it perhaps two dozen times. Only eight or nine of those surfs have been shared with anybody else. My feelings about my Secret Spot are difficult to explain. It's as if this spot – just a slab of rock, really, with a few feet of water on it at low tide – is a sacred site, a kind of personal Mecca.

If I were to be completely honest, I'd have to say that nothing, not my family, not my bank account (ha!), not my country nor even my species, brings out quite the same combination of feelings – a weird mix of selfishness, dedication and worship at the altar of the surfing experience.

Recently I admitted as much to a non-surfing friend. He looked at me as if everything he'd suspected about surfing and surfers was true. "So", he said, "you go surfing at this place for a few hours a year?"

"Yes."

"It's usually pretty cold and windy, right?"

"Yeah, usually."

"And like in summer there's probably thousands of people on this beach and they can all see the place?"

"Yes."

"But it's a secret?" My friend, a civilised, intelligent human being, was stunned at this bizarre leap of logic. It was as if we were suddenly speaking different languages. How could I explain the fact that I felt like I owned something I couldn't possibly legally own; the fact that I constantly tried to avoid telling people where this surf spot was, despite wanting constantly to tell them about how great it felt to ride waves there?

The simple fact was – I couldn't. Irrational behaviour in the face of a Secret Spot has defined the actions of hundreds, probably thousands, of surfers in the past 30 years, and it's given rise to a unique set of rules – a kind of Code – by which surfers alone operate and which only surfers truly understand.

Elements of this Code are peculiar and often contradictory. For instance, most people who know a Secret Spot have been introduced to it by somebody else, yet the first thing that person does is to swear them to utter secrecy as to its location. In other instances, surfers who were first attracted to a Spot through a magazine article will often become the Spot's most savage defenders, doing all they can to prevent any further publicity. For a few surfers, like the guy arrested recently in California for breaking the ribs of someone who'd pulled up at "his" Spot, the Code even licenses acts of violence against transgressors.

Yet this Code, irrational as it may sometimes seem, and the image behind it – the dream of the Perfect Wave – is an enormously powerful force within the surfing mythology. It has penetrated every area of our sport. It's used to sell everything from magazines to wetsuits.

More important, and more fascinating, it has become part of an intricate moral fabric which underpins the lives of dedicated surfers worldwide – a fabric which in its own way is as dense as any woven by the Catholic, Muslim, Hindu or Jewish high priests of the world.

Like the moral foundations of so many religions, the Code of the Secret Spot can be seen to have developed in distinct stages: one, which we might call the "Garden of Eden" or "Genesis" stage, during which a kind of purity and innocence reigned and no wrong could be done, for there was no wrong to do; two, the committing of Original Sin and the casting out of humanity, soiled by its own corruption; three, a world of confusion, where people struggle to live by laws that seem straightforward but can be bent to suit a need; four, dreadful to contemplate, the End of the World.

Genesis

The core of it all can be seen in that most primitive of all surfing urges: the need to Travel. I say "travel" as distinct from its currently far more popular cousin, "tourism".

Tourism is to do with recreation; a tourist is essentially on holiday, taking a break from a life led somewhere else.

A traveller is something else: the word implies a life led in pursuit of something, a life lived literally on the road.

In the 1950s and early 1960s, rogue surfers were one of very few groups of humans – others being America's early motorcycle gangs, Beats and proto-hippies, and scientific mavericks like Jacques Cousteau – still truly engaged in Travel.

The reason surfers first travelled goes right to the heart of the counter-culture and its emergence following the Second World War. "I think it's like everything – someone does it but he doesn't know why he's doing it," says Peter Troy, one of Australia's original nomadic surfers, whose outrageous exploits on the road have become a matter of legend. "I don't think there was any particular reason [for travelling]. Not to escape a crowd, there weren't any. No-one went away looking for secret places. We were all totally innocent, we didn't know anything about drugs and hippies or anything."

Troy dates his travelling days back to the late 1950s.

"I was brought up in that era when there was a breaking away from black-shoes-white-shirt-tie and off to work. We didn't necessarily know why we should break away. Society was saying we should go to university and get a job and be good."

Peter tried, spending five years in a Melbourne accountant's office while telling all his mates down at Bells Beach how he was going to Hawaii next winter. He also tried making surfboards in his spare time, but there was no money in surfboards. He failed his accountancy exams. "In my subconscious I was trying to make an escape."

Finally he made some money showing surf movies at Melbourne's Dendy Cinema. Peter took the money and got on a boat for the then Mother Country, England – a weird destination for a surfer, but "I was too scared to do anything else", he says. He went to the Channel Islands, found surf, followed his nose to Biarritz, then somehow got a crew job on a yacht bound for the US. In Hawaii that winter he walked down the beach at Pipeline, took one look, figured it was his shot at glory, went out and got his face badly smashed into the bottom.

"This made me semi-famous as that stupid Australian who got his face smashed in. I got things I wouldn't have got otherwise; I got to meet John

Severson [then owner/editor of *Surfer* magazine]. Pretty soon I got invited to go to Peru by Felipe Pomar."

It was here, says Pete, that his travels really took off: Shigi Shimada, a Peruvian surfer who later died at Pipe, took him up into the Andes and sent him off down the other side into Brazil, telling him: "Don't just be a tourist, be a traveller".

The absolute innocence of Peter's experience can be nicely illustrated by an incident that occurred on Copacabana Beach in Brazil. Troy was walking on the beach, groggy from amoebic dysentery, when he saw ahead of him a kid carrying what looked like a brand new surfboard. It was the first board he'd seen in Brazil; he raced up to the kid, who happened to be the son of the French Ambassador to Brazil and his father had bought the surfboard on a recent trip overseas.

"Come on," said Peter, "I'll show you how to ride it", and together they headed around to Ipanema, where a small left was peeling off the corner. Peter went out, caught a few waves, and within minutes had attracted a yelling, 500-strong crowd.

Today, Brazil has one of the world's biggest and most active surfing populations; at the time, Peter couldn't possibly have known what he was starting. He was taken in by a family and nursed back to health, in return teaching their kids to surf.

"I didn't really go looking for secret places," he says. "I'd follow these rivers down to the smelly old ocean and find myself walking along the coast wondering if there'd be some surf. Well, you keep doing that one day you walk around a corner and go shit, there's a good wave."

In this way, crashing through the 1950s and '60s, Troy and others like him came across truly unknown surf spots: waves like Lagundri Bay on Nias, Grajagan on Java and Puerto Escondido on Mexico's mainland coast. But in many ways, these original travellers didn't even pick up on the importance of their discoveries. The guys who came next weren't just travelling; they were looking for Secrets.

Exodus

As the 1960s merged into the '70s, the well-known surf spots, both on the USA's West Coast and in some parts of Australia, were crowded; tension infiltrated lineups from Malibu to Bondi. It was this occurrence – waves becoming scarcer – that drove surfers further and further afield, now actively on the lookout for new places to ride waves.

When I was a kid, growing up innocently middle-class on Sydney's northern beaches, I loved the idea of these surfers who struck out into the unknown, suffered torments, and finally arrived at their own versions of Heaven. They seemed like shamans, prophets driven half-mad by a diet of locusts and honey out there in their own private deserts. They would up and vanish one day, then stumble back into town six months later, sunburned, malarial, missing teeth, a stone lighter, but with a light in their eyes that spoke of waves beyond my dreams. They were True Believers, they lived the word of the Gospels, and I was sure they were willing to die that way too.

But there was a price they paid for this belief. They had gone to the edge of the earth and come back with a Secret, yet they were now to live in torment, in thrall to the Secret.

Some stuck to commandment number one of the Code and chose never to tell, only to find others discovering their spot and spreading the word. Others, following the logic of the American gold rushes of the 1850s, sought to stake a claim at a Spot: in effect, to take possession.

This idea – that a surfer or surfers can claim ownership of a surf break – goes to the very heart of our moral Code. Nobody owns the waves, it is said. This may be true in a strictly legal sense, but is it true on the deeper moral level? Many surfers who've spent years of their lives learning the curves and moods of a powerful and alluring surf spot feel a sense of ownership that makes land-based property rights seem feeble by comparison.

Over the years this has led to healthy developments in the sport, particularly an environmental awareness that sets surfers apart from any other sportspeople. It's also led to some really weird, fascinating stuff: holiday surf camps; battles over access to coasts as far apart as Sumatra and California; and primitive, ferocious acts of Spot defence.

Some places became notorious as getaway spots for refugees from soiled humanity. Margaret River in Western Australia, home of the classic ex-Bondi surfing iconoclast Robert Conneeley, was a big hit among expatriate Americans, as was NSW's Byron Bay. Ironically, both are now prime real estate. By 1979, many of today's legendary spots – Grajagan, Tavarua, the Australian north-west – had been discovered and surfed numerous times. The 1980s would be the decade of the Surf Camp.

In the early '80s you could pay US$100 per day to stay in Mike Boyum's camp on the jungle fringe at G-land, which had been discovered in 1970 by a friend of Boyum's, Bob Laverty. This was a time when there really were tigers strolling through the camp at night, when the supply boat might not arrive for a week in solid swell conditions, and if Boyum decided you weren't the right sort of person, you didn't get in. Today there are two camps at Grajagan; between them they have no problem in holding the 150 surfers, staff and media associated with a major professional surfing competition.

Tavarua, founded by Americans Dave Clark and Scott Funk in the mid-'80s, has gone in 10 years from a rat- and snake-infested desert island to the world's best known surf camp, where surfers pay up to US$165 a night to stay in little three-bed *bures* (huts) and surf the fabled Restaurant Reef and its close neighbour, Cloudbreak.

This is Surf Tourism at its most obvious, and it's often derided by the few hardcore adventurers who remain out there on what fringes they can still find. But the origin of the surf camp phenomenon can be found in a very practical reading of the Code: a reading which suggests this may be the best way to preserve at least a little of the original Secret Spot experience.

The theory was recently explained to me by Captain Martin Daly, of the *Indies Trader*. "See, you've got to make a choice," the Captain told me, as we drifted at anchor recently just off a location known in 1990 to less than a handful of people; now two other boats were anchored nearby, and the spot has two or three different names. "Once you've found one of these spots, you've got to figure that someone else is gonna come along and find it too. Now eventually that means more and more people in the lineup, crap everywhere, surf slum on the beach, the whole feeling of the place disappears. You can let that happen or you can try to keep some kind of exclusivity – try to make sure not too many people surf it at once, and they get to feel like they're having something special."

It sounds good, at least until you look at some of the undeniably weird incidents that have sprung up around surf camps in the past few years. Mainly these have had to do with competition for "rights" to a location – in effect, disputes over Ownership. Journalist Tim Baker once wrote a hilarious article in *Australia's Surfing Life* about a visit to Fiji with Steven Turner, a surf camp operator trying to get access to Cloudbreak. Suspicion of their motives got so high, says Baker, that "the Tavarua people had us followed. There was this little Indian taxi driver following us around, taking photos. It was bizarre". On another occasion, a deportation order was issued against Sydney surfers Rob Bain and Scott Somerville when they tried to set up a camp with similar access; Bain and Somerville simply avoided the authorities until it was time to head back home.

Competition has even invaded Captain Daly's Indonesian wonderland. In 1997, a charter company known as Great Breaks, Inc., run by Western Australian businessman Rick Cameron, claimed exclusive rights to charter control in the area. This proved over time to be a red herring; but since then, some 20 boats booked through at least three world-wide surf tour operators have played cat and mouse around the island chain, sometimes cooperating to minimise crowd effects at the well-known breaks, sometimes not.

Today, it's hard to imagine Captain Daly's feelings, 15 years after he first surfed the fabled Lance's right, as he pulls his boat up to the sight of over a dozen surfers in the water. "I try to be mellow," he says, "a couple of times I've paddled out here and known that none of the guys in the water have any idea who I am or what the place means to me. I just think about the days I've had it perfect with just me in the water."

Protection by enclave is another way in which small groups of surfers have tried to preserve the Secret Spot. At the "Ranch", just south of California's Point Conception, wealthy landowners have blocked road access to perhaps the finest surfing coast in the main-land USA. Buying a piece of land on the Ranch, or being personally escorted by a landowner, is the only way through the gates.

Many less-well-off surfers from nearby Santa Barbara access the Ranch coast from the ocean by small boats, but even then there's a strict Code as to which are "Owners' Spots" and "Boaters' Spots". (The cream, naturally, belongs to the owners.)

The Ranch smacks of a nasty élitism, but in fact it works: the coastline remains pristine, and a good day's surfing there is filled with an extraordinary sense of serene beauty. It's hard to overestimate the value of such things in the context of ultra-urbanised Los Angeles-San Diego, a region crushed by the worst coastal over-development on earth.

Californian surfer Dave Gilovich, with whom I did a Ranch run in 1993 (and who doesn't own land on the Ranch), summed up the ambivalence he and many Californians have toward the place: "On one hand it sucks that not everyone can surf here. But on the other hand, if it means the coastline is preserved, maybe that's an acceptable sacrifice."

Other places have become violent, locals suddenly hurling the Code out the window and turning feral in defence of a break. The finest example of this in the modern world is surely Lunada Bay in the Los Angeles area. Lunada Bay is an extraordinary place in the annals of Secret Spot morality: a sort of surfing version of the Middle East, where religion is turned upside down to serve some base human need for territory. It is a right-hand reef break peeling into a small bay on the furthest outskirts of a wealthy residential enclave known as the Palos Verdes Peninsula, which juts out into the sea almost directly west of the social night-mare that is south central Los Angeles.

Many years ago Palos Verdes was a happy hunting ground for some of American surfing's founders, the likes of "Doc" Ball, Leroy Grannis, Dr Don James, and, later, Da Bull himself, Greg Noll. But during the mid-'70s, the vibe at Lunada began to get weird. Stories spread that if you went surfing at the Bay, you risked having rocks thrown at you, your board broken, your car tyres let down, or maybe all three at once.

Some older locals say the invention of the legrope, around 1975, was what sent things off balance.

"Before then, the rocks (along the shore) were crowd control," Zen Del Rio, a born-and-bred Bay surfer, told *Surfing* magazine in 1992. "Once the leash was invented, it was open market for people lacking enough surfing and swimming experience." Attempts by injured parties, including a Brazilian surfer whose rental car was damaged in 1994, to pursue the Lunada locals through the police generally met with little response; the Palos Verdes police force is funded through fees paid by the residents, and they didn't want outsiders encouraged to visit their enclave.

Eventually a civil case was brought by Los Angeles surfer Geoff Hagins against Bay local Peter McCollum. McCollum, 35, who'd been filmed threatening Hagins and his nephew at Lunada by an LA television crew, lost the case, theoretically opening the way for a legal enforcing of the right to surf – which is about as far away from the Code as you can get.

In such ways through the past two decades the mythology of the Secret Spot has grown richer, stranger, and more firmly rooted in our collective picture of surfing. But the Secret Spot itself has grown rarer, and in the process it has become more valuable – which means the Code is constantly being bent to suit the needs of the user.

The Oracles
There can be no doubt that surf magazines, and surf

media generally, have played a pivotal role in scripting the moral landscape of the Secret Spot.

Just as the much-assaulted "meeja" does in a wider societal sense, surf media provides a lightning rod for everything from salivating perfect-wave fantasy to furious letters from "locals" attacking the latest photo-spread of their spot.

Many years ago, surf mags urged surfers to visit new spots the mags had found. Looking back, there's a marvellous innocence about such mags, published at a time when Secret Spots were still unnecessary. According to the modern moral mosaic, they were in fact committing the Original Sin.

How much effect do the magazines really have on locations? "I've heard an argument for not even naming the well-known places," says Tim Baker, a former editor of *Australia's Surfing Life*. "Mark Cunningham [the Pipeline lifeguard/bodysurfer] says that every time you name Kirra, Pipeline, J-Bay in a caption, you're reinforcing the idea that every surfer's got to surf these places. I don't think I'd go that far. But certainly as I've got older I've grown in the appreciation that it's good for people to work to find surf spots." Imagine! The Presbyterian work ethic, resurfacing in a most unlikely arena.

Through the post-hippie 1970s, magazines like *Tracks* and *Surfing World* sometimes deliberately misnamed spots in order to throw curious readers off the scent. Today, under simultaneous pressure to find and expose new spots and to somehow enshroud their exact locations in an alluring haze of mystery, surf magazines tread a strange and sticky path, sometimes respecting the Code, other times stepping far beyond it.

I have to admit here to a soiled history. In several years as editor of the US-based *Surfing* magazine, I authorised publication of a couple of articles that creamed even the most liberal interpretation of the Code. One in particular – a beautiful photospread of a remote, never-published Californian pointbreak – was a colossal misjudgement, stemming as much from my inexperience with the US version of the Code (very rigid, very fundamentalist) as anything else.

People called the magazine, threatening explosions, death by shotgun, and all kinds of wild retribution. I could deal with that; but a couple of letters really got to me. They came from highly-committed surfers who clearly felt at least as strongly about this spot as I did about my Secret Spot 10,000 kilometres away in Australia. "Man, it feels like you've torn my heart out," read one of the letters. "(The Spot) is sacred, and I wonder if you would have done this if you had spent time here yourself. I feel betrayed by a fellow surfer."

This letter, more than any threat, made me cringe: I'd broken the Code, and a fellow surfer was calling me to account.

Steve Hawk, former editor of *Surfer*, the self-proclaimed "Bible of the Sport", sums up some of the moral confusion inherent in his job. "On the one hand I wanna turn people on to surfing," says Hawk. "I think the world would be a better place if more people felt that sensation. But at the same time..."

He cites a great example of how tangled the Secret Spot morality is becoming with a story of photographer John Callahan's recent trip to New Caledonia: when one of the trip surfers wanted to give a board to a local grom, the boat captain dissuaded him from doing so, saying it would only help to create a hostile local crew some point down the track.

Hawk says of his time at *Surfer*: "We didn't have any hard and fast rules. They're [the spots] all so different. If there's an indigenous population of local surfers, then we were more likely to take them into account and respect their rights. I kind of let the writer and photographer dictate what should happen since they were the ones who had the contact with the place." Iceland, far into the northern hemisphere, for instance: "I'd have no problem showing a map of the island with every spot detailed. There's only three surfers living there and they were totally stoked to see our crew. If there's no locals there, who's to say we can't name it?"

This sounds great in theory, but in practice it leads to constant flouting of the Code.

Philippine spot Cloud Nine was literally unknown until it was published in the March 1993 issue of *Surfer*, leading to a situation Hawk describes as "pretty radical, I mean there's surf camps there now". Recently *Surfer* broke an internationally respected "no-names" magazine code on an Indonesian island chain from which some of the best travel articles of the past few years have emerged; the magazine followed its latest piece with a trade-off tourism ad – "Win a free trip to....!" – naming each spot and the island chain itself.

One time Hawk sent photographer Bob Barbour on a trip to Oregon, where he scored beautiful waves at a little-known beachbreak. Barbour was on the beach shooting when a couple of the notoriously-hostile locals fronted him, demanding to know what was happening to the photos. Barbour told them the shots weren't going into the magazine; subsequently of course they ended up in a cover story. Hawk got a call: "What the fuck, man?"

"I asked the guy, 'So let's get this right, you threatened the photographer? Told him you were gonna beat him up if the photos were going to a magazine?'

"'Yeah, that's right, man.'

"'So he lied to protect himself from violence?'

"'Yeah.'

"'And now you're calling me to complain? Well, aren't you a pinhead!' He was the only guy I've actually hung up on."

Hawk – now editorial director of California-based surf Website Swell.com – is a smart guy, a former newspaper journalist who's grown used to popping off the sound bite for other journalists.

Yet he is bedevilled by the inconsistencies of his role in the intricate moral interplay of the Secret Spot. He grew up as a surfer entranced by a famous photo hanging on a friend's wall of a surfer paddling out at Cojo Point in California's Ranch coast, and claims it remains his favourite wave; yet recently a Ranch landowning friend was verbally attacked by another Rancher for bringing Hawk on a day's surfing trip. "Mostly I will sacrifice quality for solitude," he says, stating a habit of heading south at Huntington Beach, away from crowds at the Pier, despite the slacker waves.

"But I haven't surfed any real secret spots, maybe that's why I don't empathise that much with those guys."

A fascinating way in which Secret Spot mythology has come to serve many masters can be seen in the rapid rise during the 1990s of what might be termed "soul" advertising and marketing within the surf industry. From Quiksilver's incredible never-ending Crossing boat trips, to Billabong's Super Challenge out on the once-sacred West Australian desert coast, even to the everyday surf company trip chasing advertising photo fodder through Indonesia, the industry's pursuit of a "soul" feel has meshed so finely with the goals of the surf media that the lines between advertising and editorial are often blurred beyond recognition.

By far the most prominent of these campaigns has been waged on behalf of Torquay-based Rip Curl under the banner, "The Search".

Doug "Claw" Warbrick surfed Angourie on what may have been its second day ever ridden. The year was 1964, a week or so after Midget Farrelly won the World Titles at Manly Beach, and a contingent of surfers, both Aussie and foreign, were making their way up the NSW coast on a post-contest surf safari.

Perhaps 20 or 30 of them got to Crescent Head; then Bob Evans, the legendary surf flick maker and *Surfing World*'s owner-publisher, got hold of Joey Cabell, Rod Brooks and a couple of other hotties, and split for this spot they'd heard about from Bob's fisherman brother Dick. All Claw heard was the name of a town: "Yamba".

"There was myself, Dick Milich, Ian Miller and one other," recalls Claw. "We followed maps up the Pacific Highway and somehow or other we got there. Joey and those guys had got there a day earlier and surfed it already. After a couple of days Bob and his crew moved on, I'm not sure where they went. We just stayed there and surfed it by ourselves."

Nearly thirty years later, Claw, by now the co-owner/founder of Rip Curl, among the world's largest surf industry companies, was on a completely different trip – this time in a boat off Sumbawa, Indonesia – to launch one of the most successful marketing campaigns in modern surf industry history.

Thus was mounted The Search. This was – and is – "soul" surf marketing at its most aggressive. It comprised a seemingly never-ending worldwide video shoot, originally spearheaded by Derek Hynd and US filmmaker Sonny Miller; the hiring (until recently) of Tom Curren to an exclusive contract, along with a group of surfers – Frankie Oberholzer, Byron Howarth, Pancho Sullivan and, most recently, Hawaii's Tamayo Perry – whose sole task was to free-surf for the Search camera crews; and perhaps most radical, a magazine ad campaign that featured no Rip Curl products at all, but a series of empty waves at nameless (occasionally doctored) locations.

"We wanted to show we had a broader appreciation of the sport," says Claw. "We recognised that pro surfing was not the only form of surfing and some aspects of pro surfing could even be offensive to the average surfer.... Anyway, we went on the Sumbawa trip with all the management people and we talked about our direction, thinking then that we might de-emphasise the pros and look at other, purer aspects. We were just out there, surfing, looking for new little reefs, I mean we were actually living the real surfing life at the time, and we decided that this is what we should be showing people."

Apparently by coincidence, one of the great post-Bob Evans issues of *Surfing World* was a classic travel issue – volume 27, number 3, published in 1978, and named on the front cover: "The Search".

Claw says he can't recall that particular issue: "It might have been in our sub-conscious."

SW's publisher of the period, Bruce Channon, says he and fellow publisher Hugh McLeod were "mildly amused" by the Rip Curl campaign's key phrase. He has never discussed it with Claw.

In the interests of theological research, I asked Claw if he could give me a rundown of the Code as he – a surfer of 40 years' standing, who has more than a few western Victorian Secret Spots up his sleeve – saw it. A few days later, he sent me the following list by fax:

1. Only take the people you are surfing with at the time, i.e. travelling in your car or staying at your house, etc., and provided that:
   a) They will keep quiet about the wave's location, quality and conditions, or better still, say nothing to anyone ever.
   b) If they are photographers, journalists or travelling

pros you need to be sure they are sworn to the above and that they will not in any accurate way identify the spot ever.

2. Never reveal information about secret spots to anyone you are not actually surfing with at the time.

3. Always respect any local surfers and/or other surfers in the know, especially when they are surfing the break. Further respect any local codes they keep themselves.

However, never give ground to blatant bad vibes or aggro, because at the end of the day no-one has exclusive rights to any wave. The ocean belongs to all surfers, especially those prepared to search and endure hardship to find and surf them.

(That Presbyterian work ethic again!)

In 1998, in an example of perfect post-modernist irony, Rip Curl declined to renew the contract of their highest-ranked ASP WCT pro, Shane Powell.

The reason? Powell, in his own words, was "burned out" on the Search and wanted some time to train and concentrate on his world championship goal. Going on location simply to ride perfect surf, Peter Troy's stroke of luck, the Adventurer's goal, had become – a job.

Armageddon?

And thus we approach the End of the World, the inevitable day when every surfing coast of note will have been explored and laid bare, and the image of the Secret Spot will finally exist in image only. Once, in the glory days of Eden, this must have seemed impossible. Today, well, surf mags are forced to visit the Arctic Circle to find unridden waves, and Internet communications technology permits live surf contest Webcasts from nameless Indonesian islands and barely-ridden Tahitian reef fringes.

A Net Surfcam updates a view of Jeffreys Bay,

South Africa, once every 15 seconds. Airfare to Europe used to be 23 times the weekly wage back in 1960; now it's about three weeks' worth. There will be no more Travel; merely Tourism.

"I think to some degree the western world is losing its hardness," says Peter Troy. "Surfing has got a lot easier. Discovering Nias took me eight months on a motor-bike. For most people the hardship of adventure has been taken away... People go to Bali as if it's a trip from Sydney to Terrigal.

"I could name you a hundred secret places and the only reason they're still secret is because people won't put the effort in. They've got two weeks' holiday, they want to pay the money and be somewhere their meals are prepared for them."

With the untouchability of a great prophet, Peter goes right ahead and names 'em, these spots; Frigate Island in the Seychelles, Baquerizo Morena in the Galapagos, the Ha'apai island group in Tonga, and what he calls "the ultimate" – Parson's Point, the southernmost tip of Great Nicobar in the Indian Ocean, above Sumatra. "And nobody will go there. The islands are closed to foreign travellers and to get there you need to get permission from the Indian Government in New Delhi. And they won't give you permission! I went all the way to Delhi with a letter from the Prime Minister of Australia, they took one look and said that's a lovely letter, you can't go." He laughs delightedly at the idea.

Peter has his own judgement on the issue, and perhaps that will be the way of the future – perhaps Armageddon will leave us stripped naked before Huey, forced into our private purgatories on the Code of the Secret Spot.

Personally, like I said, I'm torn. Part of me is a Shi'ite Muslim, a fanatical defender of the Faith. I don't want 30 people joining me out at my Secret Spot, getting in the way, showing no respect for the wave and its circumstances, putting on their little attitudes... But something in me is pulled toward Alby Falzon's somewhat higher moral ground. Somebody from one of the US mags called Alby recently and asked him about Bali.

Alby is the guy whose amazing movie "Morning of the Earth" painted the extraordinary first screen images of Uluwatu and fixed the haunting image of that great Indonesian staple in the minds of thousands of surfers. The mag guy wanted to know: in the light of Bali's current state – perhaps the most tourist-exploited Third World state on earth – does Alby have second thoughts about having released that footage?

"I told him I had no problem with it at all," says Alby. "People should be shown things. It's all about raising their consciousness. There's six billion people on this planet, they're here and they're not going away. We have to share things."

Postscript
A shorter version of this piece, entitled "Defending the Faith", originally appeared in *Deep* magazine, Australia, in 1998.

TRIBAL PISSINGS

Gunter Swoboda

Gunter O. Swoboda is a psychologist who started surfing 28 years ago on arriving in Australia from Vienna. Aged 12 he immediately took to the water with a passion that has continued unabated. Since then he has surfed about every possible board and spends most of his free time in and around the water. In his working day on the Northern Beaches of Sydney, Gunter spends much of his time with the consequences of both overt and covert violence. He is now taking the issue of violence and its causes and consequences one step further by working to put it firmly on the social agenda.

"Once upon a time some of the people took to the ocean, firstly to fish and survive from the wealth it had to offer, then to travel and trade for goods, and, soon, to find new lands to settle. Some of the people began to ride the waves and it was good."

Hang on, that's not how it is though. As I write this part of the story of violence in a sport that supposedly has a history of reflecting a laid-back and chilled-out lifestyle, caring for the environment and with a certain spiritual overtone, I am also aware how far from the truth this often is.

So what gives with the aggro and violence?

As a psychologist, I am interested in why and how we do things and the way we do them. I frequently have to deal with the consequences of violence and this is of great concern to me. As a result, I've spent a lot of time trying to understand both victim and perpetrator. Surfing is a way of life that I cherish and therefore violence in surfing affects me directly. Most importantly, I am interested in looking at what we can do to get a handle on this bullshit behaviour.

I know that we actually have a pretty good idea of

what contributes to the increase in violence. We also have a good idea about what we can do about preventing the frequency and the severity of violence. I think a lot can be explained by thinking about this in terms of what binds people together, like by thinking in terms of tribes. After all, we often refer to ourselves as a tribe. It also means taking a look at how we relate to competition, how we cope with change and what the consequences of these issues are. Similarly it is also about relationships, parenting and the media.

Since the early days of surfing, those who took to the ocean did so for many different reasons and came from diverse walks of life. The love of the ocean and the thrill of riding the waves bound those men and women together. Once the bond was strong enough we came to see ourselves as a new tribe. With the idea of the tribe came the ways by which you were known as a member of the tribe; it had to do with where you surfed, the clothes you wore, the music you listened to. You knew people, people with influence – and in surfing that was people who surfed well, made boards and, if you were a gremmie, those who had a car. Tribalism meant localism. Your beach was yours and that of the other locals.

Also, like in all tribes, you needed to be socially upwardly mobile. How did you achieve this when material possessions – other than your board and maybe an old bomb of a car to get you around – mattered little?

Well, you worked on your surfing; the better you surfed, the higher you sat in the chain of authority and status.

In the beginning, the conflict and threats to the tribe came from the outside. Society, particularly mums and dads – although often awed by the skill required to tackle the ocean – also saw surfing only as a sport, something that you did in your spare time. To them, surfing was *not* a way of life.

They felt that you couldn't earn a living from it and that eventually you had to grow out of it. The words "You won't be able to do this for the rest of your life" rang in most surfers' ears from a very early age on. Most of us believed that; some of us rebelled, for better or worse.

My dad recently asked me what I had been doing; I said "surfing". To which he replied, "Isn't it time you gave it away?" This was from a man who had spent most of his life in and around the ocean.

Eventually, as a surfer, you also faced dangers from other tribes: like bikers, clubbies, teachers, the cops and anyone else who objected to your existence.

Conflict and confrontations grew, but you knew your enemy, or at least you thought you did. The tribe had grown and, as a result, you felt strong; others would help to fight the enemy. But as you looked out to sea, you saw more of the tribe and they had begun to surf things other than the board, and the waves became crowded and your brother became your enemy. The threat had moved to the inside. No longer could you be sure who was friend and who was foe. There were mats, kneeboards, shortboards, long-boards, goat boats, skis, and bodyboards. Boards became attached to surfers by ropes. Change was happening quickly and inevitably and there was nothing you could do about it. Your sense of power and owner-ship diminished.

Our tribe has territory, one that at times needs to be defended from either real or imagined threats. Real threats are generally environmental. Territory means resources. In our case, it's waves. Resources are limited, threats are increasing, and tension rises. In this it's no different to any -ism. Like nationalism, it creates an "us and them" situation in which the "them" is never as good or as right as we are.

And so the competition gets more intense. Competition is even more attractive today than in the past, because the stakes are higher and therefore the gains are greater. Unfortunately, attitudes are less than tolerant. As a result of the rapid changes, the growing numbers and the shrinking resources, aggression has increased and so, therefore, so has the violence.

A big issue is the competition for waves. There are more people now but the number of breaks – and therefore the number of waves – is pretty much the same. So one of the main issues is that of resources. We are over-crowding the available breaks. This is where localism/tribalism kicks in, because it's now about ownership. This leads to surfers becoming frustrated because they feel pushed out and threatened by others and may feel and think that they are getting fewer waves.

It's at this point that we go from the social issues to the individual surfer.

Now, frustration in itself is not a problem. Good mental health and living successfully means being able to deal with frustration. Nat's accident in '64, when he cut his foot before the contest, is a good example of suc-cessfully dealing with frustration. Frustration becomes a problem and eventually leads to violence only when the surfer has difficulty in lowering the level of that frustration.

Being able to reduce frustration has a lot to do with what you experience in growing up.

We know that most people who resort to violence have generally learnt that it gets you what you want and that it's also a good way to hide your own insecuri-ties and feelings. More often than not the person has seen someone they love and admire use violence as a way of dealing with difficult situations.

The first thing to remember is that all of us have a little system in our head called the "fight-flight mechanism" that activates when there is something in our environment that we think can hurt us, like another surfer. This system is designed to get the mind and body ready when either you need to defend yourself or you need to get the hell out of there. The system provides you with a rush of adrenalin that prepares you for the worst.

We don't really need something that makes us aggressive to the point of being violent when the "threat" is not life threatening. And that threat could simply be the size of the surf. So if that six-foot swell takes you out of your comfort zone, and you feel scared, then the next sort of threat, like someone dropping in on you, will cause an aggressive reaction and maybe even violence.

Violence, generally, masks feelings of fear and/or hurt. I learnt this clearly while working with domestic violence perpetrators and teenagers who get busted for assault. Most men who hit women and children are afraid of rejection and the feeling of powerlessness. In order to maintain their sense of security, they try to control other people by the use of violence. Unfortunately most men are unaware of what's going on for them emotionally at this level and therefore just react.

An added problem the violence-prone person/surfer has is that they tend to act first and think later, frequently regretting their actions and often feeling remorseful, yet having difficulty in accepting that they were wrong in using violence. They'll justify what they did, rather than say sorry. There are also people who use violence in a very calculated and deliberate way, who will feel no regrets or remorse about what they are doing. Generally – and luckily – they tend to be few and far between.

These people also tend to want things immediately. When they don't get what it is that they want immediately, they quickly get frustrated, angry and aggressive. The final solution, if they don't feel like they have got what they want, is to use violence.

The picture now gets a bit more complicated because when someone who is aggro confronts other people, they get scared and one of two things can happen: they can avoid the aggro person; or they can begin to identify or relate to the aggro in order to reduce their own fear or anxiety.

What follows then is a pecking order or food chain of authority and status, in which the most aggressive person is at the top and the least aggressive person is at the bottom. You can see this in groups of boys where, by and large, anti-social behaviour gets you in the good books with the other guys.

Gangs also operate on similar principles. As mentioned earlier, surfers traditionally have also hung out in groups and the same stuff operates with us. We have a social structure, rules and behaviours that relate to who is the most dominant, which frequently is defined by who is the "best" (most aggressive) surfer. Ideally, if you're going to use aggression, then use it in relation to how you tackle the wave. When crowds are large and waves are few, then the aggression is often focused on any perceived threat, in most cases another surfer – particularly the one who is seen as an outsider or someone who has broken one of the rules.

So we have a situation in which the group influences the individual and the individual influences the group. What this influence looks like depends on the choices we make collectively and individually.

The elders of this tribe are re-examining their own attitudes and behaviour and looking closely at what values we are going to promote in this and future generations.

Currently aggression – and, to a large degree, violence – is actually often rewarded. We need to change this.

I believe that any worthwhile lasting change has to come from an inner evolution, not a revolution or technical answers. These may help but they won't sustain us in the long term. Surfers, including myself, have frequently expressed concerns about a number of social and political issues, but I think we have been slow to look at our own attitudes and behaviour.

Again, we need to change this.

One of the major problems we have today is that our society generally is facing some major issues and the increase in surf rage is a reflection of the increase in violent behaviour generally in our society.

Individuals today face considerably more frustration in their daily lives.

The focus on material success, competition and achievement has preoccupied adults with their own needs rather than those of their children or the larger community – even like the planet itself. Most of us rationalise that we are working so hard in order to give our children a better way of life. This is perhaps true for some, but most of us choose the career path for more selfish reasons. It's difficult as a parent to give kids the time and attention they need when you're working twelve hours a day to get to the top of the career ladder.

Not having fathers around is one of the reasons for kids becoming more violent, particularly boys. However, having said that, having no father is better than having a violent father, provided that the kids have other healthy male role models in their lives. We need fathers and men in general, with the right attitude – a non-violent attitude: men who are able to give the right time and attention to their children, who are consistently loving and yet firm. And particularly those who can lead by example.

To do this, we need a society that prioritises family issues, effective parenting and social consciousness.

So what is it that I am saying about surf rage? Well, basically that it's about how I, as an individual, deal with life in general. Some of us inevitably have learnt that violence gets you what you want. Some of us have grown up with violence and will use it whenever there is any sort of threat real or imagined. But that can't be an excuse.

Similarly, social issues are important, because aggression in our society is often rewarded and there is a very thin line between competition, aggression and violence.

The big question is: what can we do about this disturbing trend?

Well, firstly we need to remember that there is never a simple solution to anything. We need to be very clear about the differences between competition, aggression and violence and how we need to deal with each of them.

Having said this, however, I believe that we are in a position to do something about the problem on several different levels.

In our society, technological solutions tend to be the most attractive and the most likely to be implemented. They require the least effort by people and are generally just expensive.

Ironically, problems in surfing are proving to be no different from any other issues in our society. We know that we can increase the number of breaks, which we have identified as one of the causes of surf rage, by building artificial breaks in places where waves are of poor quality and frequently inconsistent.

This takes the pressure off existing breaks and spreads the demand over a wider area. This solution has, however, two disadvantages: it is costly and it does not address the human factor which, in my view, is the real problem.

What we really need to do is tackle the source of the problem, at the tribal and individual level.

What can the tribe do to *alleviate* the problem? We are not going to eliminate it completely – I may be idealistic but I am not stupid.

Most kids look up to their heroes, no matter what sport they are into. They will not only want to look like them and sound like them, but they will want to act like them. Surfing's no different. As a tribe we need to provide role models that show that you can be competitive and not an aggressive and violent asshole.

The elders, and the competitors of the tribe, need to agree to show that it is possible to think before you act, even when we are in a highly competitive and charged state. Part of this means letting grommets know what the rules are.

I am constantly amazed at the persistent debate in and out of the line-up about what makes a drop-in. In almost every other sport you don't get to play unless you understand the rules.

It is also important that we teach grommets about sportsmanship. Sportsmanship is about principles that reflect respect and acceptance of each other, regardless of who we are, where we surf, what we can do and what we surf. Good sportsmanship balances rights with responsibilities and, above all, it emphasises that it's important how you play the game as well as winning it.

It is my view that our community's desperate search for answers to feeling bad has led to an excessive preoccupation with individualism and self-esteem.

Many children have inflated egos that leave little

or no room for empathy and concern for others. Psychologically speaking, we know that this leads to children becoming aggressive and prone to violence.

The result is that these kids don't tolerate being frustrated, want things immediately and, if they don't get them, use violence. It also underscores that winning at all costs is perfectly OK. Winning is what counts, not how you play the game. So if you can get more waves than anybody else can, the better you'll look; and it doesn't matter how you get them.

Kids won't learn good sportsmanship on their own; they need to be taught. This requires time – time with good role models.

The other side to this is that as a tribe we need to deal with breaches of good sportsmanship by clearly showing that overly aggressive and violent behaviour will not be tolerated, particularly among the élite of the sport.

In professional surfing, as in other sports, aggression and violence needs to be censured. So, if you get too aggro in a contest and smack your opponent in the head, you get disqualified. If you continue to do it, you get barred, and fined and, ultimately, banned.

On the other hand, good sportsmanship should be recognised and rewarded.

Individual surfers and groups of surfers can do all of this. As more and more boardriders clubs are setting up, we can, as the tribal elders, make sure that they promote the "right stuff".

We need to ask questions. Do they teach and promote non-violence? Do they teach respect for other surfers? Do they have consequences built in to the contest rules for breaking those rules? Do the competitors know and understand the consequences and how are they enforced?

This stuff should also be taught at surf clinics and

camps. We need standards that reinforce the message that aggression and violence won't be tolerated and eventually we'll get that message across.

Surfing consists of many people with the right stuff. In our history there have been many who have sacrificed something to help or assist another surfer; let's hear more from them and about them.

People like Mick Dooley, Ray Gleave, Bonga Perkins, Rell Sunn and many more are part of a positive history with a strong tradition. If we want this tradition to continue we need to be active and persistent, because change doesn't happen overnight. Let's get it together and promote what really matters: having a good time but not at the expense of others.

THE AUSTRALIAN WAY

The rules that govern Australian line-ups are extremely flexible
– if you're local.

Fred Pawle

*Fred Pawle learned to surf in 1972, at the age of 10, on the beaches near
Fremantle, Perth. Surfing initially got in the way of him pursuing any other
serious vocation in life until, at age 25, having travelled to a broad range
of remote breaks around the world, he returned to Perth and enrolled in a
BA course to pursue a career in journalism. He is now a sub-editor with
THE AUSTRALIAN (and the newspaper's unofficial surf writer).*

For three days, I've sat on the phone, nodding and
agreeing as I talk to surfers from around Australia
about the importance of respect in the line-up and the
need for violence – or at least the threat of it – to
maintain order in the water and ensure that the people
who deserve to catch the most waves, do so. It's been a
soul-destroying task.

I left my own home beach when I was 21, sixteen
long years ago. For most of that time, I've been semi-
itinerant, never bothering to settle down in one place
long enough to become a well-known face, let alone
hang out with the locals. I usually surf alone or with
one or two mates, at whatever break suits the conditions and my time constraints that day. So when I find
myself saying, "Yeah, sure, you go this one," to someone who claims territoriality over a stretch of water
just because he never left home, and demands respect
from a stranger who, unlike him, didn't grow up there,
marry a local chick and settle down a few blocks from
his parents' house, a little part of me dies.

I've learned to be humble in the water, but I'm not
proud of that. A middle-class upbringing at a beach
where crowds were never an issue set me on a laid-back,

passive path in surfing, as well as in life. Some people might think that's lucky, but it's not. To get your so-called "fair share" at a crowded beach these days means you've got to be prepared to put up or piss off.

And, if some prick who looks to be a keen fighter, with a handful of mates to back him up, takes offence at your presence, chances are you will, as I did recently, piss off. Life isn't an American movie where the good guy wins because he's imbued with an indomitable sense of virtue; and surfers don't belong to a utopian society based on perfect barrels and spiritual fraternity.

My worst experience happened at Maroubra, a beach where I once lived briefly, and still surf semi-regularly. It was about as pleasant as a weekday gets; sunny, light offshore wind, two-foot wedges over a shallow bank walling up long enough to get a couple of moves in. Nothing to get excited – or aggro – about, just ample evidence, if you need it, that it's good to be alive. Three or four locals had the best part of the bank, and I could see there wasn't much room for any-one else. I picked a spot to myself a polite distance away. After a few waves and about half an hour, a par-ticularly sweet peak loomed up in front of me; I barely had to move to catch it. One of the young locals pad-dled from ten metres away, came right alongside and did his best to drop in. I cut him off as I got up, so he sat back and tried to shove his board in my face. Paddling back out, I copped a serious stink-eye, which my wide grin probably did little to dispel. "I should have fucking poked my board in your eye," he said.

"I was on the inside, my wave," I said matter-of-factly. But human nature in the grip of territorialism doesn't accept the rules adhered to by outsiders. "Locals only", the graffiti that adorned the retaining wall at Maroubra for a few years, actually means "locals rule".

"I fucking live here, I'll have any fucking wave I want," he snarled.

What do you say to that? You have to say something. I thought I had a reasonable comeback. "That's good, mate. So you're enjoying yourself then?" I asked. The weird thing about humour is that angry people don't get it. History records that Adolf Hitler, Joseph Stalin and Saddam Hussein never cracked a single joke between them, and of all their thousands of photographs and portraits, not one bears evidence of them ever having laughed at the occasional absurdity of life. "Yeah, I'm fucking enjoying myself," he yelled, sounding a bit like Cartman from South Park.

That's when he asked me in, to settle it on the sand. I paddled off, telling him I wasn't into it. To his credit, he didn't come after me, nor did he follow me when I caught a wave in soon after, a pleasant surf spoiled by a dumb experience.

"Most of the blokes won't join in if there's a blue on," says Jai Abberton, one of the senior locals at Maroubra, and a witty, gregarious bloke to boot. "Usually, if a non-local wants a go, we'll just say, righto, one on one, let's see what you've got."

Even better, from the outsider's point of view, the fight's usually over when the victim hits the ground. "Some of the boys have done time," he says, "so they're not going to jump on a bloke because it's not worth the risk [of being charged with assault and sent back inside]."

What should be noted about that sentence is that Jai doesn't once assume that the local will be the one on the sand at the end of the blue. "But what we've got here [at Maroubra] is hardly worth fighting for anyway. I just wish we had a break like Shark Island [at Cronulla] or something. You see the waves here and you think, it's hardly worth it, is it."

Maybe not the waves, but the local brotherhood is. Maroubra can be a very special place, if you grew up there. Jai and his two brothers, Koby and Sunny, have set up a boxing gym in their backyard. The ropes of the makeshift ring are occy straps, and the local grommets get into it twice a week to spar and work out. Boxing, like surfing, is about light footwork, shoulder strength and quick reflexes. The kids have taken to it in a big way.

The Abbertons, who provide this paternalism and training free to any local kid who asks, are the next best thing to family for some of them. "We get kids from Lexington [the nearby housing estate] who are from broken families or their parents are on the gear," says Jai. "We all spend Christmas together, that sort of thing."

Nothing bonds blokes like violence. But if the alternative is misguided adolescents heading for disaster, well... How long the Maroubra brotherhood can stay in the area, however, is uncertain.

It's the last of the beaches on the city side of Sydney Harbour to be gentrified. Once a medium-density enclave of working-class hardnuts, it is now sprouting cafes and expensively renovated apartments. The long-time locals haven't been priced out of the area yet; but if its more famous cousin Bondi is anything to go by, they will be. Unsurprisingly, my conversations with old and new locals around the country found that localism peaks when the popularity of a break coincides with its surrounding suburb being at the lower end of the socioeconomic ladder. Ironically, gentrification seems to bring with it a resignation that the place isn't worth fighting for any more.

In the interim, however, another local is anticipating a hostile summer, Maroubra's first as a well-known tourist attraction.

"They've opened up a backpackers hostel at the pub," says Paul "Moff" Moffat, a Maroubra beach inspector who grew up with Jai and Sunny, and who also helps train the kids to box. His cruisy, friendly demeanour belies the determination of his localism. "A lot of Brazilians have decided to move in. A few of them have been dropping in, and the boys have had to say a few words."

Is he just being xenophobic? "No. They shit me because they come in packs, and they think they can dominate an area. Go to Padang [Bali] and there'll be like 20 of them trying to dominate the place." Is it going to come to blows? "Hopefully it won't, but maybe it will."

For all that, Maroubra is not a nasty place to go surfing.

"If you respect the locals and don't expect to catch every wave that comes through, you're going to have a good surf," says Moff. All but one of my surfs there testify to that.

What if he sees a non-local having a shocker, getting frustrated that he can't catch a wave, and one comes through that could relieve some of the bloke's tension – would he let him have it? Moff doesn't hesitate. "Nah," he says, smiling, "if I'm at Maroubra, it's part and parcel of being a local."

My experience as a long-time non-local has found that, unfortunately, the reverse doesn't apply. If a local gets frustrated, the next wave is his, whether he is on the inside or not. This is one of the variations of the drop-in rule, and one that is understood by all surfers. More than the peaceful-vibe bullshit that once defined surfing to others and even to ourselves, we are now most tightly bound by the understanding of the "fair share", which apportions a fairer share to local blokes than it does to outsiders. And somewhere beneath that come women, bodyboarders, mal-surfers and wave-ski riders.

Former semi-professional surfer Adam Koleits achieved minor fame in the mid '90s as the ringleader of a group of surfers determined to rid their break, Trigg Point in Perth, of wave-ski riders and bodyboarders. He even appeared in the *West Australian* newspaper, running over a booger who had dropped in on him. He recalls with wry amusement that the term "surf Nazi" was even bandied about by polite non-surfers morbidly fascinated by a gang of supposedly angry young men.

"I ran over a bodyboarder who dropped in on me while I had a photographer on the beach taking shots," he says. "I did the biggest cuttie on him, with his head under my board. I thought I was just gonna do it nicely, just grind my board off him.

"I didn't hurt the bloke, my board was just squeezed against his head. But a surfing magazine ran the full sequence and it looked pretty amazing. No one had ever run photos like that before. That's when *Riptide* [a bodyboarder magazine] started ringing me up, saying I was a swine. It got blown out of proportion."

Unlike Maroubra, Trigg is a middle-class suburb of predominantly young families, with no shortage of bored pre-pubescent kids and middle-aged men looking for something to amuse them on weekends. Inevitably, boogie-boards, wave-skis and Trigg Point, one of the few decent breaks in Perth, are going to beckon.

Another distinction from Maroubra is that the locals don't see themselves as a brotherhood.

"The locals here are not as tight as I've seen in other places around the world. People still look after each other, though."

They sure do. Adam and his mates used to grab a

wave-skier's paddle and throw it to each other down the line until the last bloke flung it round the back of the point, at which moment the ski-rider would skulk off, demoralised. Other times they'd tip the ski over and hold it there until its rider had to eject from his safety belt.

Adam laughs heartily as he recalls this, knowing right is on his side.

"It was hilarious," he says. "We set about trying to get them out of there. We didn't give them an inch because we knew if we did the next day they're gonna come back."

As for bodyboarders: "We've stemmed the flow of the whole thing, made it not as welcome as it could be. There's a hell of a lot of beach there, it's better for their craft down the beach, where the waves are a bit suckier. The Point is out of control still, but if we'd let those goat-boats come through, plus the esky lids, it would be twice as packed, with not one bit of respect."

Is violence worth it?

"Intimidation is, but violence isn't. I don't like it at any time. There's just times when people have got to know. When I was younger I was in on the sand a bit, mostly with guys on wave skis. I had to do a bit of wrestling and throwing around."

Adam was 13 when a mal-rider threatened to punch his head in at the Point.

He immediately enrolled in a kickboxing school, and has been looking after himself ever since. That was 14 years ago. He has no problem with competent conventional surfers. "The locals are friendly to any-one who can pull a bottom turn and do a belt," he says. "I have a different thing towards other surfers – we've all got to surf. But the other type of craft at crowded spots, they're pushing their luck."

Apart from the usual argument that scarce waves

should not be wasted on riders of easy-to-use craft, Adam also has the moral authority of someone who earned his spot in the pecking order.

"When I was young you had to earn your respect. You didn't just paddle out with 10 sponsors' stickers on your board expecting to get waves. These days, grommets haven't got any respect, they're skipping over that bit. They don't have that sort of looking up to the older guys. We did cheeky things but we didn't push it. I did a drop-in when I was 13 and the guy got me and threw me head-first into a glass recycling bin. If you stepped out of line in those days you expected to get a bit of payback. I don't see that happening now."

Old-fashioned respect can be easily interpreted as a type of conservatism, something that surfers, most of whom see their pastime as counter-culture and constantly progressive, wouldn't dream of associating themselves with. Talking with Adam, the conversation easily swings towards the crowding and over-development of the Margaret River area, and how the old hippies and soul surfers are being pushed further south by the rapacious march of yuppiedom.

Conservatism, at least for his own youth, seems to come naturally to him. But before he gets too misty-eyed, he zeroes in on the worst aspect of change in surfing.

"Nothing against Taj [Burrow, a West Australian who turned professional at 18], but ever since he came on the scene, these grommets all just want to be like him," he says. "They do one tail slide, at the age of 13, and they're thinking, 'oh wow, I'm the one! By the time I'm 18 I'm going to be able to do 20 tail slides!' They make the third round of a junior comp, and look out!

"I don't know where surfing is going to go if these grommets don't realise the bigger picture. You can call it localism, but these older guys have waited in line for a long time [to get a bigger share of waves]. Realistically, they do deserve it."

Adam has finally realised that nothing can stop this change. After 15 years at the Point, he is finally looking further afield. "You get sick of defending something for so long. You see so many nightmares that you've just got to go and surf the outer reefs. Consistent crowds, guys consistently going over falls in front of you, all that can get to you. You get a bit worn out, and think, 'I gotta escape from this'."

Adam has splashed out on a jet-ski and, with a few mates, surfs the isolated reefs kilometres offshore from Perth, where the only respect expected is from sharks. This, of course, is far more relaxing.

It's all a matter of perception, which broadens with age. Mark Rabbidge has been surfing for 40 years, mostly at the intensely local North Narrabeen, including during the heady late '60s, when cars were sometimes torched and the locals were a tight-knit group of seriously hot surfers.

He, his wife Pam Burridge, son Michael and mate Peter Townend recently surfed Kirra Point on a good day, when the crowd was ridiculously thick.

"Within 20 minutes the four of us were back on the beach," he says. "We were all saying you can't ride it. There's too much flotsam and jetsam in the way. And we're all capable surfers – two of us were former world champions."

"Then I'd watch these guys pull up, look at the waves, and they can't get in their wetties and into the water quick enough. What they're seeing is the waves, but what I'm seeing is the crowd. You simply couldn't ride the wave for all the people in the way."

You want to know the real source of violence in the water?

Mark, a rational and thoughtful 51-year-old, has a carefully considered opinion on the subject, based on his own experience. His mum was sick when he was an infant. He was born a Protestant, but his father's family, where he was sent to be looked after, was Catholic, and didn't much like their little foreign interloper. He was often belted, and was a miserable, neglected infant.

"At 14, I turned into a wild sort of guy," he says, "and that's when people get pigeonholed. Twenty-six years ago I was mad. What I had was a reputation, and when you've got a reputation any young bloke wants to take it apart.

"When you lash out, you lash out through fear. When people scream and yell and fight, it's not that they're saying, 'get out of my way'. They're saying you don't know what it's like to be me."

Having mellowed, Mark is now reasonably flexible about the rules governing who gets the next wave. He understands the "champion arrogance" of some surfers, who are psychologically driven to drop in, even when the greatest expense is their own.

"I saw Tommy Carroll do it during the Pipe Masters, when it cost him a world title," he says. "It's the personality of a champion. It's about being so good that you think that everyone else is gonna waste what you'd do with the wave."

He says localism is closely related to tribalism, and that's not a bad thing.

"I firmly believe in the importance of localism," he says. "It should be seen as a proud thing."

These days, Mark uses it to smooth things out for others. When he sees a non-local getting frustrated at Green Island, his new home break on the New South Wales south coast, he'll tell the bloke to drop in on him if he can; if so, Mark pulls out and lets the bloke have it. That sort of generosity, though, is only extended to those who respect Mark's authority in the line-up. It also requires the merest empathy, something that most surfers think they simply can't afford to possess.

"Education of being aware of other people in the surf is the problem. There's no fixed rule," he says before relating his own version of conservatism. "I'm finding it increasingly difficult to deal with life, having to deal with all this shit. When I was young you'd smack them in the face and it would be over. The blues wouldn't last a long time. It'd be over. It's all right if you just leave it in the water. Just don't take it to the beach with you."

It's at this point that my investigations start to get a bit weird.

Like most of the militant locals I have spoken to, Eric van Druten, 41, is happy to chat about his brand of localism. I listen for over an hour while he rationalises the need for heavy locals, sometimes contradicting himself, and explains the mood in the water at his break, one of the best point breaks in the world, Burleigh.

"Is it all right for locals to drop in on outsiders?" I ask.

"Depends on the person's competence. If you're a competent surfer and someone drops in on you you'll get around it if your competence level is high enough. Just surf in behind him. That goes on constantly.

"That's where it comes back to people sitting in the water sussing each other out. Locals don't fade each other. But if that fella's ability is good enough and he deals with it without reacting verbally or physically, we'll stop doing it. If he deals with it, he gets respect quicker than a loudmouth who's got a good surfing ability.

"Locals burn holiday surfers. But if you can tell he's a good surfer we won't do it again. There are one or two people who will. I'll drop in at any opportunity but I don't do it in a dangerous manner. If I know him it's fun for him to try and get out of that situation. As long as you're not in the tube.

"But you've got to verbally state yourself. You gotta yell if you're in the tube nowadays. You've still gotta pay a price now by yelling, you can't just sit back in the tube and enjoy yourself – you've gotta yell to stake your claim."

I call a friend who moved to Burleigh more than a year ago, who says Eric dropped in on him while he was in the tube only that morning.

Another Burleigh local, Dwayne Harris, laughs when I say Eric shows respect to competent non-locals. "That might be his interpretation," he says. "Maybe he just sees dropping in as sharing."

Dwayne puts it succinctly enough: "Basically we all share it. It's pretty mellow these days. If you go out there and mind your own business and don't have an attitude, no one's going to hassle you. It was worse in the '70s and '80s, the laws were a lot more lax then. These days you can't hit people. You get sued. But that's not why you go surfing anyway."

Eric's logic might be a bit scattered, but eventually he tells me something that illuminates his aggressive need to get his "fair share" at Burleigh. Surfers like to think that their experiences are unprecedented, that everything they do is so new and exciting that it is beyond previous human experience. But Eric, without realising it, draws an analogy to postwar Holland, where his family came from.

Eric's grandfather owned a pub, and during the war, under the Nazi occupation, turned his hand to selling gin on the black market. When the Nazis were defeated, a power vacuum was created, and communists rushed in to fill it. They went around appropriating the property of people who had survived the occupation. Eric's grandparents and their nine children did the bolt to Australia.

Eric learned to surf at Dee Why, Sydney, in the late '50s, where his family would spend all day on weekends hanging out on the beach with the Dutch community. To them, the freedom of Australia was amazing. But to Eric, the freedom of surfing was even better.

He left school at 16, found himself on the Gold Coast and hasn't left. He started a family young (his eldest daughter is now at university) while maintaining an intense love of surfing.

"I come from a heritage of bondage," he says. "Twenty-five years down the track I find I still just want to go surfing. I do it for love. I never competed, I never joined the boardriders. I never wanted to do anything but go surfing. That's the greatest gift I can give my kids, is that kind of freedom.

"A lot of Australians don't appreciate that."

Eric used to voluntarily coach kids, too, back in the '80s. "That's when surf schools were free, and were sponsored by companies like Milo. In the old days you gave surfing to the kids because they loved the ocean. Now the coaching clinics want money, and people get what they can from surfing because they've paid for it like a ride at Dreamworld. They don't teach people etiquette. Now, people want a return."

The irony, though, is that Eric's habit of dropping in on non-locals at Burleigh is not a million miles from communists banging on his grandfather's door in Holland, saying, "Bugger the rules, what's yours is mine. Now piss off."

I've got my own form of conservatism to add to this debate, based on something that happened to me in the mid-80s in Rabat, Morocco.

I was there in summer, and scored hardly any

waves. But one day I saw guys out at a bank next to a breakwall in the huge harbour. From the distance, they looked like ants on one-foot waves. Stoked that I'd finally found waves, I grabbed my board, caught the ferry across the river, ran through the old market and sprinted out along the rocks.

When I got there, a group of local grommets were hanging out between sessions, and there were about ten of them in the water, enjoying a very nice four-foot peak. They were not good surfers, but they were undeniably as stoked as any groms in the world.

I nodded g'day and sat down to put on my leggie while everyone sussed me out. I paddled out under barely-disguised close scrutiny. Eventually, one of the groms paddled over to me and asked where I was from. When I said "Australia", they all smiled with relief. They were just worried I might be some French prick who'd come to hassle them off their waves and abuse them, which apparently is the French custom down that way. Every one of them paddled up and shook my hand.

These kids were, to a grom, riding boards previously left behind by travelling Australians. We shared the waves, enjoying them in a way my home-bound compatriots probably wouldn't understand. I arranged to meet one of them later that arvo, and gave him the spare leggie I'd brought. When I think about it now, I wish I'd attached it to the board I was riding and given him that, too.

I haven't been back, but I suspect progress has infected even this bunch of happy locals. It happened in Indonesia. It's bound to happen everywhere.

I don't look back on that rare experience as showing "respect" for the locals; respect is one of the most over-used words in the English language. It usually means one person or group imposing a dubious set of standards on someone else, usually at their expense. I don't go surfing to show respect to anyone. I go out to enjoy myself, and am prepared to do it while causing my fellow surfers the least amount of grief. Being a perceptive kind of bloke, I can quite assuredly say that I know who has more fun.

Anyone who demands respect just doesn't know how good it can get.

CALIFORNICATION

The home of modern surfing is at the forefront of surf rage.

Mike Kew

Mike Kew is only 25; he grew up surfing in San Diego, California, moving to northern California where he continued surfing while completing degrees in journalism and English. Seeing the whole picture through young eyes he was perfect for the task of reporting on Surf Rage in California. Mike likes to think of himself as a global local; he currently ranges throughout the world as an ambassador of stoke. Surfing is his life, and always will be.

One of the bad legacies of Romanticism was this greedy prizing of one's own solitude in an increasingly crowded nature. The central conceit of the "traveller", as distinct from the mere "tourist", was that he was alone in the landscape: its sole, original discoverer.

To this end, the travellers' books became engines of mass destruction. They exterminated parties of hikers in the Hindu Kush, wiped out convoys of tour buses, disappeared the cheerful caravan of motor homes, assassinated park rangers, and left a world ethnically cleansed of everyone except the writer and his dusky native friends.

Jonathan Raban, *Passage to Juneau: A Sea and Its Meanings*

If it were only thus in Southern California, aka "SoCal", the birthplace of modern surfing.

Essentially one massive sprawl from Santa Barbara southward to the Mexican border, few people visit here without drawing some notion that, hey, this would be a pretty damn nice place to live. Jobs are abundant, the weather's hard to top, and there's pearly-white sand beaches.

Hence, the landscape that many romanticise as a

Mediterranean utopia exists today as an over-populated concrete jungle, saturated with construction, traffic jams, urban transplants and ... ever-thickening swarms of surfers.

Let's face it: the water's relatively warm, the waves are mostly small and forgiving and there's bikinied chicks on the beach, with ample lifeguards to rescue your ass should the need arise. What could be more conducive to Joe Blow's concept of the Beach Boys-Surfin' USA fairytale?

To many, however, the beaches of Southern California are a steaming circus-like meat-grinder, stuffed with millions of people, imported desert sand, palm trees, sweaty policemen, uptight and overworked lifeguards, clueless tourist hordes, plastic women, suffocating smog, thrashed ecosystems, endless parking meters, spotless SUVs, neon lights, squalid bums, fast-food wrappers, polluted ocean water, screaming children, toxic bonfires, cigarette butts, broken glass, shit and stale urine.

Augment this with what *Surfer* magazine's Steve Barilotti christened as the "Hollywood of surfing" and you have one very crowded place for wave riding purposes.

Naturally, as with all flourishing animal species and their respective territories, the resources sought and cherished by Southern California surfers dip into a perpetually-slimmer stockhold while the influx of newcomers fails to cease and the residential developers rise to the selfish demands of human overpopulation.

For the most part, the sea prevails as one of the last true escapes from the horrors of society, yet localism – deemed by many to be the bane of surfing – is one microcosm of human behaviour that seeps out from the pavement and into the lineup. One SoCal refugee claimed it's a matter of "not enough nature to go around" and that it's "too many dogs after the same food". One native San Diegan referred to it as being "too many cocks in the chicken coop ... there is always someone who wants to rule the roost".

This is nothing new, of course.

"The term they use in Europe is provincialism," says John Elwell, 68, a legendary world-traveller, comrade of men like Pat Curren, Bob Simmons and Flippy Hoffman, and lifelong resident of Coronado. "The provinces all have local customs and prejudices ... another term is territorialism – each pack claims territorial rights. What creates the problem is the lack of what they seek, jealousy or just being different. Too many individuals invade the other's territory for the same thing ... this is a primitive instinct and why gangs fight for turf. (Tom) Blake and (Tom) Zahn encountered it in Hawaii."

Perhaps the earliest outline of surfing localism was actually weaned in Hawaii, as recalled by Blake in a 1989 interview with historian Gary Lynch: "You roamed around there – nobody knew you, and it's a wonderful way to live, when you keep a low profile. Like, nobody's shooting at you, you know? That went on for years, and it's just, like ... I got interested in their sports – surfing and paddling – and managed to build a little better board than they had and beat them in their contests. And then they began to look at you: 'There's something we don't like.' And that was the end of the real good days."

As Elwell put it, "If you look too good, expect to get pecked by the jealous assholes."

Yet, as anybody who has attempted to surf Malibu or Trestles on a sunny summer Saturday knows, it is the common kook who invariably creates pile-ups and tension, which reflectively escalate into stink-eye, verbal insults, and, in the rarest cases, physical violence.

"The kooks are the guys who get in my way – the ones who are stealing waves from me," Miki Dora would say in his July 1965 *Surfer* interview. "They're all thieves, taking my waves."

Dora, stepson to Gard Chapin (who was said to be the best surfer on the coast during the late 1940s and early 1950s) certainly wasn't the first famous surfer to exhibit aggressive tactics in crowded Southern California lineups. Chapin himself was quite arrogant and vocal, not well-liked, but immensely respected by guys like Bob Simmons, the legendary innovator who emulated Chapin's aggressive tactics in the water.

"These two guys [Chapin and Simmons] yelled a lot as they were coming down [the wave]; they expected respect," Elwell said. "Chapin got away with it, but Simmons was the apprentice and got bashed, dunked, and stoned. There were threats, of course, and I remember when Simmons spat in Joe Quigg's face. That carried on for scores of years – we're talking like 50 years of bad feelings over that. Chapin was very aggressive, very arrogant. He thought most surfers weren't very good anyway, and he told Bob that. He said, 'We'll just run over them, yell at them.' And so here's the mentor telling the younger guy, and, of course, Simmons knew this guy was one of the best surfers on the coast, everybody says he was, except he had a terrible attitude. If a person feels superior and they're arrogant and they're pugnacious – they like to fight – that's one of the problems.

"None of that ever occurred down here [in San Diego]. Guys were gentlemen; they helped younger surfers. Younger surfers also had the respect to stay out of a better surfer's way. Another case with Simmons was at San Onofre, and it (was a result of) collisions. People were in front of him, and they deliberately were run over. The design of boards had changed.

They were much more manoeuvrable and much faster. They were overtaking surfers on a wave. And so these guys are coming across again – what do you do? Here's a guy just coming down on you fast, and you're in the way. You have a board that you can't manoeuvre – you know, a big plank – and so, eventually, Simmons and Chapin ran over them, and they had fibreglass on their boards. So their boards were damaged and they're mad – and some of these guys were big guys – the plank surfers – a lot of them were bigger athletes. Simmons got punched and the board fell down on him. A lot of people thought it was kind of funny, but Simmons didn't have that problem here at all. There was nothing that ever occurred. Down here, we stayed out of his way. But we're talking about late '40s and early '50s, when no one else was exhibiting this behaviour except a few people at San Onofre.

"Bob was aggressive and caustic with his language, and he was a deep part of the problem. The other thing is, you say, well, what are these guys doing taking off in front of a guy who they know has a faster board? Now, the other story is the same thing happened at Palos Verdes. Bob hated these big – what they called the 'kook boxes' – the big, square-sided paddle boards. They couldn't manoeuvre them. They could just stand up and slide on them. He got in the same situation, you know – 'You're in my way.' And of course, they're saying, 'Hey, we're from Palos Verdes, and you're coming up here.' So it was so nasty that they waited for him when he came up the trail. The story is that they stoned him; they started throwing rocks at him. We're talking about a guy with a very strong Scottish background, and he's angry, and he has vengeance, so he comes down there late at night with this great big adze, and these guys didn't haul their paddleboards back up the cliffs. They figured no-one was going to touch them, and no-one ever did. But Bob went down there at night – he knew where they'd put them – and he just bashed the decks in and everything else.

"Simmons was displaying this behaviour even at Hermosa and these areas where he surfed. So when he came down here, he said he didn't like LA. He said it was smoggy, and he said those guys up there had a bad attitude. He said he came out of the water and some-one had taken a can of shaving cream and shaving-creamed his whole car up. But he came down here and he was idolised at Windansea and idolised at the Sloughs. He wasn't in a popularity contest. Down here, we had a lot of respect for the better surfers, and you knew that if he went for a wave you'd never want to get on the outside of him, and you couldn't get on the inside of him. So you let him have the wave and stayed out of his way. And when we had his boards, that solved a lot of problems. We now had boards that were as fast as his, and we could ride right with him, and give him plenty of room. But that may have changed his behaviour because he had such bad results from it."

San Diego as Fight Club

A broken pelvis? A lacerated liver? Broken ribs? Six days in intensive care and ten weeks of recuperation? All because of a dispute over a barely waist-high wave? This was the case in September 1994 at Del Mar, in central San Diego County. Encinitas resident Bob Greene, 48, landed in a hospital's intensive-care unit after Spring Valley's Kevin Tiffin, 27, rocked Greene's world karate-style after complaining of being cut off on a wave by Greene. When Greene dropped in, Tiffin cracked the shits, so Greene offered to settle the dis-pute in a mature fashion on the beach.

But instead of a reasonable chat followed by an

apology and a handshake, Tiffin went ballistic when the two reached ankle-deep water, inflicting the afore-mentioned injuries while Greene's 12-year-old son watched. Tiffin's 47-year-old uncle, Kenneth Empey, a retired martial-arts teacher, barked out blow-by-blow instructions to Tiffin during the lopsided altercation. "I thought I'd go over and defuse this thing," Greene later told the San Diego Union-Tribune. "I figured we'd discuss it."

With Empey's coaching, Tiffin grabbed Greene's hair and bit into his hands and the side of his chest before slamming Greene onto the ground and kicking him repeatedly while Greene surrendered. Despite a few blows thrown by Greene, this was what the deputy dis-trict attorney said "pushed the altercation beyond the threshold of mutual combat and into a criminal act".

Empey and Tiffin fled after the incident, but Empey blew their cover a week later when he questioned a Del Mar lifeguard lieutenant regarding Greene's status. After Empey nervously admitted to being present dur-ing the assault but refused to give a witness statement, the lifeguard immediately grew suspicious. Rounding up a four-man surveillance team that tracked Empey to his car a few blocks away, a sheriff's detective nailed him. Tiffin surrendered to detectives in Encinitas that after-noon. The two accused men were booked on charges of felony battery, then released after posting bail.

In court two months later, they were ordered to stand trial in January 1995. Tiffin was sentenced to six months in custody at a work-furlough centre, which meant he could go to work during the week but had to stay at a lock-down dormitory at night and on week-ends. He also wasn't allowed to surf anywhere north of Torrey Pines State Beach (which lies just south of Del Mar) for his three years of probation. Empey was let go on a misdemeanour battery charge.

Ironically, Tiffin and Empey's home towns – Spring Valley and Lakeside – are about 20 miles inland from the beach (East County), whereas Greene resides in oceanfront Encinitas. So who's the local? Was the fight really an act of localism? Sounds like another imbecilic account of the dark side of human nature to me.

Which draws us way back to 12 January 1981, during a chest-high swell at Carlsbad's Warm Water Jetty, when a guy speared another guy with his surfboard and ultimately ended up in court. The assailant was convicted of assault with a deadly weapon, where the "weapon" was his surfboard, the first case of its kind in California.

Among the surfers out that morning were Larry Richards, a Carlsbad newcomer, and Steve Cram, a guy who'd lived and surfed in Carlsbad for most of his life. Cram took off on a set wave only to get snaked by Richards, who pulled out after realising he was in front of Cram. Richards nabbed the next wave and rode it to the inside where Cram was standing in chest-deep water. As Richards cruised by Cram heaved his board at Richards causing him to fall and be gouged on the forehead by the nose of Cram's board. Stunned, Richards demanded to know why Cram had done such a thing. Cram replied that because he was a Carlsbad local, he'd spear anybody who cut him off.

Soon afterwards, Richards executed a citizen's arrest with the aid of lifeguards. Cram heckled Richards while the lifeguards issued Cram with a citation and a notice for him to appear on criminal charges for battery. The case was assigned to Stephen Anear, a San Diego deputy district attorney who happened to be a hard-core surfer. A three-day trial in May 1981 ended with Cram's sentence of probation, a $US500 fine, and order to fund Richards' medical costs.

Another fabulous example of surf rage was an incident in March 1996 involving two 20-year-olds: one who thought he owned the beach and the other a mere visitor. La Mesa's Michael Berrill was sitting in the water at Ocean Beach when Mira Mesa's Justin Holly paddled up and told Berrill to split since Berrill wasn't a "local", even though the two boys were acquaintances while growing up in Point Loma, which adjoins Ocean Beach. Unpleasant words were exchanged, so the two hit the beach and proceeded to hit each other. Five or six other young surfers encircled the boys, all rooting for Holly. A witness said Holly threw at least eight rapid-fire punches and kicked Berrill, who suffered facial cuts and bruises before lifeguards broke up the fight. Holly attempted to skip out on the scene by paddling south towards Sunset Cliffs, but a police helicopter spotted him. Officers were waiting on the beach when Holly came in.

"I was scared," Holly later explained, "because usually the person who wins the fight gets into trouble." Holly was arrested on misdemeanour battery charges for being the aggressor, only to be cited and released since the city jail was filled to its capacity and couldn't accept misdemeanour suspects.

A mistrial was declared the following December after the jury reached an impasse. "Locals Only – that's what this case is about," said prosecutor Lisa Flaig in her opening statement. As part of an agreement with the city attorney's office, Holly later pleaded guilty to disturbing the peace and was charged under an ordinance which bans fighting in public and challenging another human to fight. He forked out $US400 in fines and received three years of probation.

As if once wasn't enough, young Holly found himself in a similar predicament (thus violating his probation) in May 1998, only this time he was partnered with his father, John Holly, 54, and older brother John Holly Jr, 24. The setting was Abs, a thick left-hand reef at Sunset Cliffs where a San Diego lifeguard by the name of Michael Pugh, 31, and his buddy Thomas Vaughn, 34, were reaping the goods of a new swell. The Hollys stroked into the line-up and sparked a confrontation on the grounds that Pugh and Vaughn were "kooks" who shouldn't surf at a spot which, according to the Hollys, was reserved for locals only. Pugh didn't quite agree with this, so the Hollys engaged the men in a battle of watery fisticuffs. The kids socked Vaughn while daddy attempted to spear him by yanking his surfboard under the water and letting it shoot forward, gouging Pugh's noggin instead. Mother Nature then stepped in with a big set, scattering the lively ensemble.

Justin Holly and his father were arrested and jailed on felony battery charges. In the courtroom, the Hollys naturally pointed the finger at Pugh and Vaughn insisting the pair triggered the tussle with a little stink-eye. When all was said and done, the Hollys pleaded guilty to misdemeanour battery charges and were ordered to dish out $US400 apiece in fines and complete a 20-hour anger-management course plus several days of community service.

Deeming Justin Holly's sentence as being far too lenient for his second offence in two years, the Sunset Cliffs incident gave San Diego lifeguard chief Chris Brewster the initiative to author and propose the California Open Waves Act. If adopted in Sacramento (the state capital), Brewster's pitch would class surfboards as deadly weapons and stiffen penalties thrown at localism perpetrators. If the Act does indeed pass, dudes like Justin Holly and Kevin Tiffin could find themselves sitting high and dry for a while.

Act excerpts:

"The state of California hereby declares that the ocean along California's coastline and the waves which strike it are an invaluable asset which is owned by no person and available for equal use by all."

"... any conviction wherein the act was accomplished during an attempt to intimidate or prevent another person from exercising lawful use of ocean resources, including but not limited to surfing ... shall include a mandatory period in custody ... of not less than 30 days for a first offense."

"... no person, regardless of residence, lineage, social status or other reason may lawfully claim the right to a wave, waves or wave break area along the California coastline."

"... a surfboard is a deadly weapon when used in an attempt to injure another person."

Said Brewster in a *Surfer* magazine interview: "The main thrust of the legislation is to proclaim clearly to all that the waves in California are a public resource open equally to all. Also, it sets up penalties for localistic intimidation and/or injury." Is this the answer for California localism? Could it curb self-righteousness and flared tempers? Might it cause guys like Holly and Tiffin to think twice before they clench their fists? Let's hope so.

The City of Angels?

Los Angeles. Hell-A. Smell-A. Draped in smog, lathered by concrete, saturated with cars and humans. Several dirty beaches west of downtown LA – once a rural haven for scoring abalone and lobster, for sunbathing, surfing, diving, swimming – have deteriorated over the years into convenient public sewage outlets, gaudy boardwalks, gang warfare turf, scenes of countless crimes, and, in the case of Long Beach, a brackish basin of foul saltwater, thanks to the US Navy's now-useless breakwall. And yet coastal LA County would be all puke if it weren't for the scenic Palos Verdes Peninsula and the odd classic (albeit polluted) point-break like Malibu, which, on 27 September 1994, was the setting for one of surfing's most ludicrous examples of surf rage.

The occasion was the Oxbow World Longboard Championship. During Joel Tudor's morning quarter-final heat, a San Fernando Valley kneeboarder/tile contractor named Richard Ernsdorf drifted into the contest zone. On the sand were Lance Ho'okano and Joe Tudor (Joel's father), who both decided to wade out and tell Ernsdorf to mosey on down the beach, away from the competitors, so as not to screw up the heat. In front of the press and hundreds of spectators, Ernsdorf reputedly grew belligerent and took a swing before "things got out of hand", Joe later told *Surfer* magazine.

Except for the very beginning, the entire scuffle was filmed. "I was upset," Joe told the *San Diego Union-Tribune*. "I didn't have the best manners." The trio exchanged blows (Ho'okano socked Ernsdorf 17 times) and Ernsdorf was motored to the hospital with a concussion, a dislocated shoulder, and several facial cuts. Felony charges were pressed against Joe and Ho'okano, although Ho'okano initially didn't return from Hawaii for court appearances, resulting in a $US250,000 warrant for his arrest. If convicted of battery and assault with great bodily injury, the men faced a possible seven years behind bars, but the charges were later reduced to misdemeanours. In addition to three years of informal probation, Ho'okano and Joe were ordered to complete 300 hours of community service, yet Joe ultimately lost the family house in the end – he took out a mortgage on his home to cover his legal fees.

"I still believe I did the right thing," Joe said. "I just didn't realise I was going to run into some psycho total jerk. It'd be like if you were at the Olympics and your daughter was out there ice skating for the gold medal and some clown decides to jump onto the ice."

Then you've got the renowned Lunada Bay, a rocky, horseshoe coastal indentation with a good right point break at its north end. Capable of holding swells of up to 20 feet, Lunada is one of the few bona fide big-wave spots in Southern California, and it's also one of the few places where the local surfers manage to make the six o'clock news.

For years, a victim's code of silence protected the already-sheltered "Bay Boys", an odd clan of trust-fund surfers who inhabit wealthy Palos Verdes Estates. All grown men, they'd behave like fifth-graders and harass visiting surfers – hurling pebbles, waxing windshields, deflating tyres, flapping their mouths like xenophobic freaks.

Most outsiders would hear of this stuff and simply surf elsewhere, saying there was no reason to deal with such hassles. "It's been known among South Bay surfers that you just don't go to Lunada Bay ... unless you know one of the regulars and they let you," Tim Dornberg, a member of the Redondo Beach Harbor Patrol, told Surfer.

But the shit started hitting the fan once David Hilton was arrested and charged with attempted assault after a Brazilian surfer snitched on him in January 1995. The Brazilian was circled by 15 Bay Boys as he and two of his buddies eyed the surf from the cliff top. "They told me if I surfed there, they would break my face, break my sunglasses – things like that," he told Surfer. So he split and came back with three Palos Verdes Estates police officers. Hilton was in the water by that time, so the Brazilian stroked out to identify him while the officers watched with binoculars. Hilton paddled furiously toward the Brazilian as if he was set to kick some ass, so the cops summoned the Redondo Beach Harbor Patrol, which bolted to the scene in a 24-foot patrol vessel. The Harbor Patrol forced Hilton to head for shore, where he was subsequently cuffed.

Two months later, Torrance's Geoff Hagins, 40, along with Mike Bernards Jr, John Hagins Jr, Charlie Rigano and Dan DiSanti (all teenagers), convinced a television film crew to join them on a trip to Lunada Bay in the hope of snagging some of the Bay Boys' antics on tape. In an interview with *Surfer*, Hagins described his intentions: "The Palos Verdes people come into Torrance, and they always bring their video cameras and nobody hassles them ... I thought, 'Well, we'll go surf Lunada Bay, and we'll bring our video cameras and we'll see how they react.' I called the people at Channel 13 (KCOP) and explained the situation, and they agreed to send the film crew ... I didn't know if there would be any Bay Boys there, but I had an idea those guys would do something. To tell you the truth, I didn't think they'd be stupid enough to do it in front of a TV camera, but they did."

Upon arrival, Hagins and the film crew were met with a handful of Bay Boys, who demanded an explanation. While Hagins went surfing, the TV guys offered the Bay Boys a chance to talk about localism, but were ultimately badgered. "It was very territorial and ridiculous," the KCOP cameraman told *Surfer*. "Some of the guys were pushing the camera and putting their hands over the lens. One guy grabbed the producer's arm. They were definitely threatening all of us."

In addition to a $US350 fine and two years' probation, Bay Boy Peter McCollum was eventually slapped with a misdemeanour assault charge after what ensued.

In *Surfer*, Hagins explained: "We were coming up the cliff when McCollum grabbed Charlie Rigano by the shoulder and twisted him around. He said, 'If you ever bring a TV crew again or try to surf here again, this is what will happen.' And then he took his fist and was slamming it into his palm right next to the kid's face, so close that from my angle, it looked like he was hitting him. This was a 36-year-old guy threatening a 16-year-old kid. What (the TV crew) filmed was McCollum up on top harassing the Bernards. Here was a big guy yelling at these little kids. I don't know if they used that video during McCollum's criminal trial, but it looked really bad."

KCOP aired a short segment of the footage that evening. "Since the thing was on TV, I've gotten hundreds of calls from people who have had problems with these (Bay Boys)," Hagins said. "We want to organise. We want to go to Lunada Bay and show them they can't do this." McCollum, whose inheritance entitles him to the Palos Verdes Estates club card, cast the whole skirmish as a provoked frame job for the otherwise innocent Bay Boys. "... (Hagins) brought a camera crew and instigated the whole thing," he told *Surfer*. "They came down here beating their chests, saying they were gonna take over. Well, we couldn't just roll over and let them. They came to my front lawn and said they're taking over, but now I'm the thug ... Yes, it's a public park and everyone has the right to play there. But we already had a game going. They can't just take over. We're protecting this place to keep it pristine for future generations."

What future generations? The Bay Boys' kids but no-one else's? A public California beach-cum-private Palos Verdes Estates fraternity?

"If this place was ever opened up, it would be packed with low riders, guys in VW bugs," McCollum told the *Los Angeles Times*. "The rocks would be marked with graffiti, and the beach wouldn't be safe at night."

To top it all off, Hagins filed a $6 million claim against the City of Palos Verdes Estates for its supposed condoning of the Bay Boys' behaviour, though the city manager called Hagin's claim "vague" and "unfounded". Hagins felt that since zero measures had been taken to thwart the Bay Boys in their 25 years of known tomfoolery, the town was going along with it to keep the beach "clean". In the end, a settlement conference was staged two months before the case was scheduled to go to trial, and McCollum agreed to pay $US15,000, which was divvied up between Hagins, the four teenagers, and one of their fathers. McCollum also scored a restraining order banning him from "harassing, intimidating, vexing or annoying" any surfers around the Palos Verdes Peninsula.

Although the case was shut, Hagins wasn't exactly jumping for joy. "Money was never the issue here," he told *Surfer*. "Public access to a public beach was the issue. After all I've been through, I would have liked to see McCollum and the City of Palos Verdes brought to trial, but it would have cost a lot of money. Those guys on the hill declared war on outside surfers in the early '70s, and we'll have to see if things have changed. I think surfers from outside of Palos Verdes are still afraid to go up there because they don't want the hassles. I do think we got the city's attention, but we'll have to see."

Hollywood-by-the-Sea
The west end of Oxnard abuts the Pacific Ocean by way of Silver Strands, a mile or so of quality beach break framed by two jetties. Claimed to be "one of the best winter surfing spots in California" and "one of localism's

last outposts" in Jack Waterman's "Fair Warning" piece, which appeared in the July 1986 issue of *Surfer,* Silver Strands has seen repeated instances of territorialism, ranging from keyed cars to group punch-outs.

"... the majority of the locals are territorial zealots crusading to halt outsiders from invading their turf ... these surfers are viciously bent on protecting their territory," Waterman wrote. "If you arrive at (Silver Strands) wearing your conventional surfwear, out-of-town surfboard and sequin-cluttered faggot wetsuit, you can count on a hassle."

Waterman then relates the ethos of local Lee Ross: "All they are doing is protecting what's theirs," Ross said. "How would you like a bunch of homos infesting your backyard?"

One of the veritable long-time ring-leaders of the surly Oxnard coterie goes by the name of Zorba, which is derived from his past practice of attaching razor blades to the nose of his surfboard. His nickname morphed from Zoro to El Razor Zorb to Zorba, and in the 1986 *Surfer* feature, at age 20, he offered this story: "I remember one time when these five big dudes from some college frat came out onto the beach with their southern surfboards. Well, I'm standing there by myself, but I ain't going to let these guys go without at least a vibe, so I tell them to split. They come over and surround me, all five of them white jocks. I tell them that being a ballplayer don't count for nothing around here. They start pushing me around; then some homeboys showed. We beat those dudes bad. That's what I like, man, backup any time of day. We're all family up here, and we all back each other. It doesn't matter how big they are or how many there are, 'cause we got 10,000 homeboys backing us from Scalon and La Colonia."

Questioned in *Surfer*'s August 1996 issue as an

attempt to decipher the philosophy of intimidation, Zorba claimed semi-retirement from full-blown localism tactics, citing a larger police presence and his own mollification.

Excerpts:

Surfer: You said it used to be really physical down there. Was anyone ever killed?

Zorba: No killing. A couple of people semi-drowned. Some cars burned. Numerous boards and fins busted out. Wetsuits ripped off. A lot of cars have been ripped off. I'm not going to say any names, or if I've ever done anything, but a lot of people have lost everything in their car: wallets, credit cards, irreplaceable stuff.

Surfer: Do you regret any of this?

Zorba: I regret hurting people, like physically. One time this guy came from outside and wanted to surf our waves. I told him I wanted to scam on his chick. He didn't like that, so I beat the shit out of him in front of his girlfriend. I feel bad about that.

Occasionally, the old Silver Strands mentality oozes onto adjacent beaches. In September 1995, Oxnard's David Ortega head-butted Mark Aaron in the chest, breaking a rib, after claiming Aaron wasn't allowed to surf at Port Hueneme Pier. Ortega, then 21, later pleaded no contest to the misdemeanour assault on Aaron, 41, a Santa Monica junior high school teacher. "We went to Hueneme for the first time," Aaron told the Associated Press. "We pulled over just north of the pier, and we were putting our wetsuits on. Within a few minutes, this guy comes over raving, asking 'Where are you from? You can't surf here'. We said, 'We're from LA.' He said, 'Get out of here'."

In May 1996, a Ventura County judge ordered Ortega to five days in jail and said he could not surf at Port Hueneme for three years as a condition of his probation. A few days after the sentencing, Ortega was caught surfing Port Hueneme, netting him six months of jail time.

The $75,000 Parking Pass

There just isn't anyone else who will be allowed to surf on the Ranch ... In the past, due to articles in your magazine and because of word of mouth, and the previous lack of security on the Ranch, a lot of surfers have come in, walked in and whatnot, to surf the beaches; and I'd like to get the message across to these people that the Ranch is closed ... I know this article is going to come out in a magazine that's read by all the surfers in the world, probably; and I just have to tell the kids – the only way they can use the Ranch is to buy a parcel and become a part of our good life here.

"The Ranch Reality", by Dick Larue, Hollister Ranch manager, *Surfer*, July 1972.

Such is the mantra which ultimately sparked the venomous owner-versus-boater feud, a breed of localism where the so-called "rights" are bought and paid for, and everyone else be damned. What the Ranch surfing tug-of-war essentially boils down to is this: throughout the 1960s, the Ranch was solely regulated by members of the Santa Barbara County Surfing Association. Since the Hollister Ranch was sub-divided in the early 1970s, well-heeled surfers have flocked and scored parcels, therefore believing it to be their exclusive right to score the Ranch solo or with a few friends, meanwhile fostering a wistful mentality that the waves at nooks like Rights and Lefts, Big Drakes, and Cojo Point belonged to them and nobody else.

Joe Hinkens' is a case in point, graciously passed on by Roger Mann, himself a Ranch local and area high school teacher:

"The incident took place in October or November of 1997. I had made several trips up to Cojo in the prior weeks and had even made the trip up the day prior to our mishap at Hollister. We would launch the Mainliner, a 23-foot sportfisher, at Gaviota and cruise the 12 miles or so up to Government Point. Our crew consisted of myself and two Santa Barbara County firefighters – Mike Dalcerri and Bill Letson.

"No more than two or three miles into our trip, as we skipped from one swell to the next, I thought I heard a bit of clatter from the engine. I immediately shut it down and noticed that the oil pressure was almost zero. After throwing the anchor and pulling the engine cover, I found the bilge to be full of oil, and the crankcase nearly empty. (It wasn't until the boat was in the shop with the engine removed that we discovered a small hole corroded in the lowest corner of the oil pan.) I had one quart of oil with me, but it didn't even register on the dipstick. We had cellular phones with us, and it was decided that I would call my wife and arrange for her to bring us some additional oil. My buddies were calling their fire station to arrange for the folks at the Hollister Ranch security gate to let my wife in.

"Ironically, it was just a few weeks earlier that many of the Santa Barbara County firefighters were at Hollister battling a brush fire that endangered several of the homes there. The Hollister Ranch contingent publicly thanked the firefighters for preventing any serious losses.

"After having made all of the arrangements, we floated lazily in the morning sun and pondered how we would get to shore to retrieve our provisions. It was a weekday, and we had not seen another boat all morning. Reluctantly, we all donned our wetsuits and hopped on our boards with the leashes tied to the bow hook of the boat and began paddling the mile or so to shore. Surprisingly, we made very good progress, but after only a few minutes, a commercial Radon came up to us, and the skipper offered us a tow to shore. We gladly accepted and, a few minutes later, we were anchored in 20 feet of water off San Augustine. There were some chest-high sets so we surfed for an hour or so before spotting my wife, trudging down the beach, dragging a case of oil in an inner tube.

"We paddled to shore and left our boards irregularly strewn several feet apart on the sand as we ran up the beach to greet my wife. After some small-talk, we thanked her and parted, with my wife heading home and the three of us walking back toward our boards, which were about a hundred yards down the beach. As we approached the boards, we noticed a Suzuki jeep driving toward us on the beach, when all of a sudden, the jeep swerved and ran right over – not one, not two, but all three surfboards! We were shocked, especially given the fact that the driver had to make several turns to hit all three boards.

"Before we even had a chance to speak, the jeep pulled to a stop, and the driver jumped out, pissed and angrily shouting, 'This is private property!' and, 'You're trespassing!' His female companion sat quietly in the car. He looked somewhat like a leftover from the Haight-Ashbury days, with scruffy grayish hair, shorts, a worn-out pair of sandals and an old, dirty T-shirt. We were equally furious – perhaps more – as we demanded an explanation. With three of us and one of him, we still wonder what possessed him to confront us and why we didn't seize the opportunity to jump him and bust his head.

"As soon as he realised who we were and that permission had already been arranged, he began to recant his story, explaining that he really hadn't seen the surfboards – you know, with the glare and all. He refused to give us his name, but we took down his license plate number and made our way back to the boat. After five or six quarts of oil we cautiously made our way back to Gaviota Pier where we loaded the boat and headed straight for the Hollister guard gate to report him. We no sooner had described the ordeal before the security guard asked, 'Was it a little red Suzuki?' He knew the guy by name: Dieter Horneman.

"We made a formal complaint that day with Hollister security, which turned it over to the Santa Barbara district attorney. After several months, we were finally notified that the district attorney was not interested in pursuing it.

"We did have our 'day in court', if you will, when we were invited to the landowners' meeting at the Ranch. The way I understand it is that this meeting takes place once a month and provides a forum for all of the landowners to gripe at one another about whatever issue is bugging them at the time. As the story goes, many of them are attorneys, so they spend a lot of time suing each other. Mostly, they validate each other's negative opinions about how boaters are coming in to surf the Ranch and spoiling their little piece of paradise.

"That whole scene bugs me. I've spent a lot of time along that stretch of coast since my first trip in 1973. I've travelled in by car and by boat. Just because some punk comes up with the scratch for a twelfth-interest in a piece of dirt eight miles from the beach hardly gives him the right to tell me how I should pursue my boating interests.

"The whole affair stirred up a lot of commotion. Eventually, Dieter Horneman was denied his beach privileges at the Ranch. The surfboards, surprisingly enough, suffered only cosmetic damage. As for boaters hanging out at the Ranch, traffic has been a little slow lately. The Gaviota launch has been down for a few years and the next closest launch is Goleta Pier or even Santa Barbara. Much to the disappointment of the Ranch landowners, rumour has it that Gaviota will be open again soon. Will localism still permeate the waves? Who knows?"

As Hinkens suggested, guys scrounge whatever bantam form of parcel possible on the Hollister Ranch, instantly gracing them with the swank title of "Ranch Owner/Local". Relative to today's price tags, *Surfer* magazine Editor Sam George dubbed it the "$75,000 parking pass".

Hollister security guard Ray Kunze, aka the Malibu Enforcer, offered an insider's perspective, one cultivated from 40 years of Ranch gravy: "A lot of boaters surf Big Drakes in the winter," he said. "And it's like, shit, nobody even knows who's the owner and who's not. I know more boaters than I do owners, and I talk to them all. Hey, I just go surf. I don't give a shit. The one thing about the whole deal is no-one owns the ocean. All they own is the access. If you drive in, you gotta go by their rules, you know what I mean? If you're a guest, you should go by the rules. Or if you're an owner, you've got to go by the rules that they've set up for themselves because it's like a big condominium. That's the way it works."

Kunze recently laid into some juice from the early boating days of the 1960s when one Ranch character named Arnie Douglas reigned – Localism Supreme (in his own mind at least). "I was one of the first boaters to go up there," Kunze recalled. "This friend of mine – Mysto George – and I were laying on the beach at Lefts and Rights and Arnie came up and started giving me shit. I told him, hey, man, just fuck off, dude. When I get warm I'll go out in the water and surf some more. I said I just got through taking orders for two years from assholes (in the Army), and I'm not taking them from you. I said I'm not breaking any law. (Arnie) was a little guy, small, short. At that time, he was like 19, and I was probably 27 or 28, and I wasn't going to take any shit off of him. Most of the guys he ever picked on were people who couldn't defend themselves. That's the way most of these surf bullies are, you know. There's a lot of guys who have come in and punched (Arnie). There's guys off boats who've punched some Ranch guys out too.

"Once, Jeff Kruthers paddled out with a machete in his mouth and Angie Reno had an oar, and they were battling each other from a boat," Kunze continued. "I always teased Kruthers every time I saw him. I'd say he'd better bring his machete because I heard Angie Reno's coming up."

Then there's the incident involving Douglas and Tracy Buell, who pointed a speargun at Douglas's face as he clawed his way into Buell's boat for a scuffle over turf rights. Buell held steady aim, ensuring that if Douglas made one more move, sharp lead would tear into his flesh. Needless to say, Douglas retreated.

Further up the Coast
A clear, balmy October afternoon on the beach at Hazard Canyon, in central San Luis Obispo County. A sturdy double-overhead west swell piles onto the reef unblemished by wind or bump, resulting in epic right-hand barrels for the tiny Canyon crew. What's wrong with this picture? To the locals, it's the sudden appearance of two-time world champ Tom Carroll in the line-up, along with Jim Banks, Indo explorer extraordinaire. The pair's Central California strike was intended to be an innocuous field-test for Quiksilver's new line of wetsuits, later to be exhibited in a ten-page *Surfer* magazine spread (August 1996) with words by Steve Barilotti.

Barilotti recalls: "I knew the reputation that it was a heavily localised place, and I just figured it was one of those places I'd rather give a pass. But since I was with Tom Carroll and Jim Banks, I figured, well, you know, I'll just fly under radar. They'll attract the crowd or the attention, and I'll just go off to the side so no one's going to worry about me. But as it turned out there was only probably about ten people out total, and spread over a wide area. So we paddled out there and some bombs started coming through. Tom Carroll started ripping, and, of course, his style was five times as good as anybody out there and basically what you had out there were a bunch of guys – semi-longboards, wearing hoods – sort of the, you know, the typical grumpy, middle-aged local, sort of pathetic creature that's hanging onto their past. But even though we were being super low-key and the cameras weren't being seen or anything, one guy took it on himself to raise a big stink and started shouting to all his friends. Like, you know, 'Who the fuck is this? Who is this, Chipper? This ain't no fuckin' whorehouse!' Because, obviously, he had seen Tom Carroll. That was the only reason that there was any notice taken at all because, realistically, there was nobody else out there. But he just felt he had to sort of piss in all four corners because these two pros had showed up. And Jim Banks is probably one of the most mellow guys I've ever known; he just kind of stayed up the point and did his own thing.

"It was weird. By the end of the day, word had gotten out. It was about a three-hour session, and some of the local guys were starting to come down because they knew that Tom Carroll and Jim Banks were there, and they wanted to meet them. The younger guys were stoked that they had a celebrity surfer down there surfing their break, but, of course, we found notes on our windows and everything: 'Don't come back here, blah, blah, blah'. But it was funny, because the young guys were apologising for the old malcontents who were there.

"Jim Banks' theory was, why are we hanging out here at (the Canyon) with these old farts, grumping and groaning like a bunch of constipated walruses, when we can just paddle 500 feet up the way and have a wave to ourselves? But Tom Carroll, being hyper-competitive and everything else, figured he could surf anywhere he wants. That's his prerogative, that's alpha male. A lot of (localism) is sort of testosterone-driven bullshit of male display and if you want to deal with that, fine. If you want to ride waves, go find a fuckin' wave."

Apparently, the Hazard Canyon "old farts" still believe it is their birthright to surf the reef with nobody but their homegrown brethren especially not with world-famous pros who get their pictures in the magazines. As luck would have it, Carroll and Banks pulled up to the Canyon on basically the best day of the year toting two professional photographers – Ted Grambeau and Tom Servais – who stealthily perched themselves high among the wooded bluffs, "their big lenses all but wrapped in camouflage netting to avoid detection," as *Surfer*'s Sam George would later note.

From the session, *Surfer* ran a one-page, ten-shot sequence of Carroll getting shacked off his nut at "Diablo's" (fictitiously renamed after the nearby Diablo Canyon nuclear power plant) plus a single photo of Canyon local and surfboard shaper Van Curaza. Soon thereafter, Curaza's cookie crumbled.

"He pretty much ruined my life," Curaza said of notorious Canyon local Jerry Grantham, who reputedly blackballed Curaza after the photo emerged. Curaza was interviewed by writer Glenn Starkey for a March 2000 cover story on Central Coast localism in

New Times, a San Luis Obispo newsprint weekly. "He screwed with my business and that affected my family ... a lot of these guys were my customers, so they became my friends, but after that photo appeared, not one of them called me to go surfing. Not one. I was completely cut off."

Starkey's *New Times* article also spotlighted on an equally comical 1999 incident at Shell Beach, up the coast from the Canyon, involving two 30-something long boarders and one mediocre wave. One guy cut the other guy off, bumped rails and ignited a brawl, resulting in assault charges and mutual regret. Paul Winje was bashed by Greg Lampert, who, claiming self-defence, regaled Starkey with his account of the fisticuffs: "He faded over [on the wave] and hit me on purpose," Lampert said. "When I confronted him, he said, 'Locals have priority around here, dude.' I told him I was more of a local than he was. I said, 'Next time you run into me we're going to go fist city.' Then he told me, 'The best thing for you to do is leave and never come back.' I got angry and threatened him. He said, 'You don't want to fuck with me in the water.' So I said, 'Let's take it to the beach.' He tried to throw sand in my face, so I beat him up."

The fight was just one of several pathetic Central Coast localism bouts over the years, a sad commentary on human nature that perhaps Central Coast-based surf historian Gary Lynch articulated best: "Two people who are unwilling to give, what has to happen – whether it be a cat or a dog or some brain-dead asshole in the water – you have to humiliate the person one way or the other, either physically or verbally. People have to see it and then that person wins and then it's okay. If you get two morons in the water it's going to be a bad situation because they have to either humiliate the person one way or the other. But it's totally a natural phenomenon that is always going to happen as long as there's humans or any animals. It's people who don't have the wherewithal to control themselves or are not intellectually astute enough to understand what's going on that the problem escalates to things like that."

So what began in Southern California as far back as the 1940s lingers into the new millennium, not surprisingly, given the sheer mass of humans and a finite resource like innocent little surf spots. Although 98 percent of SoCal surfers do exist peacefully in the lineup, several spots have a sour grape or two, and while these guys generally lay low, there are certain individuals who believe they possess some sort of rights to a specific beach. This is when words are exchanged, drop-ins and collisions occur, and the occasional fist is thrown. Boys will be boys, some might say, though most won't stand for it. Regardless, human nature won't change any time soon, and the crowds of Southern California are only on the increase. There will always be ignorance and selfishness on Earth, so my guess is that the pettiness of SoCal localism won't end any time soon. Just be prepared if you go.

Postcript: journalism equals vandalism in northern California?

It was a fine midsummer afternoon at Shelter Cove, a remote yet magical nook of southern Humboldt County, where I'd made my home for a spell. The fog had finally levitated from the sea surface, and I was itching to digest some fresh fillets. Parked my van at the usual spot down at the bottom of the boat ramp, then hopped into my skiff and motored around Point Delgada, trolling the line for salmon, lingcod or any number of rockfish. The wind and seas intensified soon thereafter, and I was having a lacklustre fishing day (snagged just one lingcod), so I buzzed back to land within two hours.

Once I neared the boat ramp, I noticed my van's windshield had been badly shattered on the passenger side, perhaps with a large stone or crowbar. Who did this? Dope-growing yokel surfers. Why? Primarily because of an innocuous, abstract piece I wrote for *Surfer* magazine focusing on commercial fishing yet containing no specific nomenclature – only generic "Pacific Northwest" and "northern California" were mentioned.

Greeted spasmodically after the issue's release with "Go back to where you came from!" and "Nice article, asshole!" by guys who hadn't even read the article, I cast it all to be rather ironic, considering I had just finished scribbling an essay for the book you're holding. Many of the Shelter Cove simpletons eyed me as a threat and were fearful of what I could do in print, i.e. suddenly exploit Shelter Cove via a 14-page extravaganza in *Surfer*. Ha!

Although I certainly minded my own business and was rather reclusive during my residency, one or two clowns seemed to make it their top priority to see what I was up to, what board I rode, where I surfed, where I boated, whom I spoke with, etc. All because I'm a journalist who thankfully wasn't raised with them. Rumours and speculation fester like disease among a myopic surfing posse of bored degenerates. They latch onto whatever dirt is being said, then draw their own negative conclusions before even speaking to someone or knowing what they're all about. One guy would invent something about me then gab to his buddies, who'd tell all of their buddies before the gossip came full-circle back to me, when all I could do was shake my head and wonder how, if possible, I could prevent such bullshit from materialising. Quite sad, really, when vibes and vandalism are hurled at somebody from the slippery foundation of ignorance, fear and bogus hearsay.

It's challenging to remain content in a place where the yokel surfers dislike and distrust you, and who do a botched job of making beach life uncomfortable, no matter how congenial you act or how much you ignore them. Lifelong isolation breeds a general misinterpretation of those who appear from afar, and it's quite wearisome trying to communicate sensibly with someone who exists in a twisted reality reaped from years of dedicated pot-smoking and a lack of real-world involvement.

"It does seem to be true that the Southern Humboldt pot culture has created some unusual people," Eureka, California-based clinical psychologist Michael Hoes, wrote after I'd relayed my experiences to him via e-mail. "What you describe is prejudicial thinking. Prejudice's strongest root seems to be ignorance. While some growers have been exemplary regarding their children's education, many have not.

"As I'm sure you've discovered, there are problems in the schools down there due to lack of family cooperation + drug abuse + lack of respect for education + lack of motivation. Their models – parents, peers, neighbors, etc. – show that one can 'do much better' by hiding out and growing dope. In the end, it catches up with them."

"Lots of dysfunction down there," Hoes continued. "Also, it sounds like these guys are not all that happy with themselves. Not much sense of meaning when you don't have to work for a living. Seems good at first blush, but most folks who I know of in this situation are not able to keep up their spirits without direction. They may be jealous of your experience and try, for that reason, to make it unimportant, by putting you/it down.

"Last, but certainly not least, when one puts his/her entire livelihood into an illegal activity (growing pot), it tends to breed suspicion. Paranoia is a way of life for some. Others become enamored with the 'outlaw' lifestyle. Dysfunctional families tend to be exclusive of strangers. They don't want anyone to find out what's going on. 'The best defence is a good offence' comes to mind."

Simply put, I inherited a bad rap because I didn't go to high school in Southern Humboldt and, basically, by existing peacefully and slicing my own groove with journalism and living with the sea. The van's windshield was easily replaced, yet some human mentalities will never change. In the words of surf historian and ex-Shelter Cove lurker Gary Lynch: "They are amoeba-brains who seek sunlight and swill for nourishment. When darkness starts seeping into the day or week or month, the only avenue of release is to find a campaign that the amoebas can rally around. It could be a new fisherman with a big, nice boat, or a foxy new gal who would never in a million years even look into their pathetic faces. And on and on. So today, it's you ... they do not understand this journalism stuff, all those words and that goddamn computer thing."

Amen.

STAIN ON THE SOUL

Glen Hening

Surfing since 1965, Glenn Hening is a teacher (history in high school, kindergarten in El Salvador, maths in East LA) and self-taught computer expert. He was working at NASA's Jet Propulsion Laboratory when he signed the papers to start the Surfrider Foundation in 1984. Profiled in numerous magazines, he recently anchored NATIONAL GEOGRAPHIC's "Save the Wave" documentary. He organises the Rincon Clean Water Classic fundraiser, and publishes "Groundswell Society", an annual publication about projects and personalities outside surfing's mainstream.

The locals had a reputation for short tempers, thuggery and a ruthless pecking order. That meant little to the invaders, whose ego-driven arrogance was fuelled by a self-image saturated with superiority. The two sides clashed in a violent confrontation. The uninvited visitors were beaten back, and the locals showed them no mercy.

Now where in the world of modern surfing did this happen? Velzyland? Cactus? Palos Verdes? Burleigh? Stockton Avenue? The Canaries? The Ranch? Narrabeen? Could be any one of dozens of intense surf spots around the globe, couldn't it?

But no, the above is not about a specific example of surfer localism per se. It's about the single most violent episode in all of human history: the battle of Stalingrad during World War II. The Nazi army had advanced rapidly for a thousand miles deep into the Russian heartland when the Soviet dictator Josef Stalin told his generals that there would be no more retreat and that they were to stand their ground to the death. And thus were revealed deep-seated human instincts of conquest, violence and revenge, resulting in the deaths of almost a million soldiers and civilians in a little less than six months.

What greater contrast could there be? Warfare to the death that destroys a city is about as far as you can get from riding aqua blue energy in warm water along beautiful coastlines, where the power and the visions provided by our mother ocean combine to make surfing an almost religious experience.

However, if our sport/art is indeed so wonderful, then "surf rage" reveals something that, I contend, is born of the exact same primal instincts that caused ten thousand deaths a day during the seige of Stalingrad. That was man at his worst, and violence among surfers, blessed as we are by nature, is pretty much in the same category.

If you think that comparing Nazis and Soviets to surfers is a bit of a stretch, then consider a story from the *Los Angeles Times* dated 26 March 2000 entitled "Drought Desperation". The article relates the story of a battle between monkeys and humans when water trucks arrived at a drought-stricken trading post in northern Kenya. When the monkeys saw the water, they attacked so ferociously that the humans were forced to retreat as the primates quenched their thirst. But the humans re-grouped and fought back against the simians with axes and machetes. Sounds like the first day of waves after a long flat spell at Sunset or Swamis or Kirra, no? And you can take the simile even one step further when talking about conflict over water: there was once a fight involving a machete at the Ranch, where gunshots have also been used to intimidate outsiders.

All this is by way of introduction to my take on what has been the single most shameful and disgraceful aspect of our sport/art for the last forty years. One has only to talk to those who have quit surfing in disgust, or those in the non-surfing public who are unable to comprehend how surfers can reveal such base human instincts when they are so blessed by the ocean, to understand how localism and violence have stained the soul of surfing.

In early April 2000 Chris Bystrom called with the idea of my writing about "surf rage" in response to the recent assault on Nat Young. His account of what had happened was pretty depressing, especially since at the time I was writing up a summary of Surfrider's Clean Water Classic event at Rincon, where we are able to run a weekend contest in great waves without security or water marshals and with the full cooperation of all the local Santa Barbara surfers.

Yet here was Chris describing Nat's serious injuries caused by a conflict in the water at Angourie. So on one hand I was filled with the satisfaction of being a part of a wonderful event where hundreds of surfers cooperated in sharing great waves at one of the most crowded breaks in the world and on the other I was sadly reminded that surfers are also capable of being reduced to the level of primates by their selfishness and lack of self-control.

Surfing is as pure a pleasure as anything we do on this planet. The beauty, the sensation and the physical challenge of riding waves are unmatched by any other sport. But surfing's internal conflicts are also unique. They affect our surfing lifestyle across the board. In fact, it seems as though our "culture" is bookended by bullshit.

At the Neanderthal end, we have our mossbacks (a deprecatory term for old, set-in-their-ways sailors, referring to turtles who've been in the water so long that moss grows on their shells). These guys never actually live at the public surf spots they call their own, but since they usually have nowhere else to go in their lives, they resent anyone showing up at "their" beach, public be damned. When intruders start riding "their" waves, they start growling with indignation like bull walruses whose cows are being eyed by rivals. They rage with jealousy as if surfing was their substitute for sex, and their aggressive attitudes lead them to commit senseless crimes of passion when they cut off strangers, challenge them to fights and worse.

At the other end of the spectrum, where professionals make their living off the sport, things are often no different. I have immense respect for Nat Young, a pioneer of advanced surfing equipment, a former world champion, a writer of surfing books and an acknowledged leader of the surfing tribe for three decades. Nat has always been aggressive in the water, and the fact that he belted eighteen-year-old Luke Hutchison after being abused relentlessly is sad but true.

Today Nat is recovering from injuries sustained when Luke's dad lost *his* sense of membership in the human race and attacked Nat mercilessly. And that is only the most recent incident among the leaders of our sport.

There is the little-known episode involving Johnny-Boy Gomes, winner of $US56,000 at a 1998 Pipeline contest organised by his friend Eddie Rothman. It was the biggest-ever first-place cheque in a surfing contest, placing Gomes at the top of the heap as a professional surfer. But only a few months later, Johnny-Boy was told to go back to Hawaii by community elders after attacking a young local surfer at a beautiful Polynesian reef.

And who can forget another landmark incident: the 1994 World Longboard Championships at Malibu. A veteran 'Bu kneeboarder didn't get out of the way fast enough when the contest started, and so Rick Ernsdorf was hospitalised after being held underwater by Joe Tudor and then having his face pummelled bloody by Lance Ho'okano.

If you consider that few, if any, veteran waveriders have not seen hostile graffiti, felt the rats-in-a-cage vibe of overcrowded surf spots or witnessed real violence, it becomes apparent that surfers all too readily reveal a deplorable strain of human character in their penchant for aggression over something given for free, a gift from nature that we use for nothing more than some momentary euphoria. We surfers forget that waves are living magic. The huge storms, the powerful winds, the great global routes of major groundswells, the graceful curve of protected shorelines and the symmetry of a wave peeling perfectly all combine to give us an unparalleled experience. And what do we do with it? For whatever reason – ego, low self-esteem, selfishness or professional greed – it becomes all too easy for surfers to ruin our heaven on earth.

How can this be? We are like true believers fighting over who will take communion, pushing and shoving and cutting in line with an infantile "Me First! Me First!" attitude as we approach the altar where our religion is confirmed. And when we finally attain the holy moment and connect with the body and soul of our faith, what do we do? "Mine! Mine!" becomes our mantra. Just ask yourself, "When was the last time you saw a pro surfer get a great wave, but then paddle back out slowly so that others could share in the same experience? When was the last time you saw a local get out of the water so that the waves would be less crowded for others? When was the last time you saw a good surfer give a kook a wave?"

Until these instincts become definitive of our surfing culture, starting with the surf industry and those making a living off the sport, surfing will suffer from a cancerous sore that won't go away. The pro tours, contests, magazines, videos, surf star reunions, big-wave exploits and guided trips to remote perfection will all mean very little until the leaders of our sport/art publicly make a commitment that says, "Enough! We leave our egos on the beach, and we enter the ocean with humility and a true sense of brotherhood." Until that day, and until the moss-backs and thugs at a hundred spots around the world wise up to what surfing is supposed to be, the next embarrassing episode of surfers as Serbians is just around the corner.

Allow me to state my credentials on the subject. I'm writing this in our family room with a view of Oxnard Shores, a place I surfed for the first time in 1968. It is not a wave for the timid when it's good. Top-to-bottom barrels unload over erratic sandbars, and you have to be in good shape to get any waves because the sets can push you up and down the beach a hundred metres at a time. Now that I have lived here going on ten years, I often find myself the first guy out at dawn and one of the few regulars when it starts maxing. So I guess that makes me a local at a place that once intimidated outsiders. Say the word "Oxnard", and the connotation among California surfers is pretty negative. But those days are over at the Shores, and that's the way I like it. I want the beach where my children play to be free of the contamination of localism, because I've seen enough of it, and I don't want to see any more.

I've dealt with several versions of "surf rage" during my surfing career in California, including Topanga in the '60s, Silver Strand and the Ranch in the '70s, and Hazard Canyon in the '80s. I've had to face it down in the water and on the beach, and based on personal experience, I've found that surfers "infected" with localism can be surprisingly vicious SOBs. They can ruin a surf spot in a way that reminds me of floating garbage poisoning the sea.

Modern surfing points to Duke Kahanamoku as its father, yet his aloha version of surfing is about as far as you'll get from the heavy scenes caused by the pools of hate that have floated in lineups around the world: the toxic spills of localism. Of course, if we as surfers look to Polynesia for our heritage, what do we do when we see a history of raids, massacres and internecine conflict throughout the South Pacific? Are we doomed by cultural genetics to duke it out over our tiny slices of paradise and the short-lived waves we ride?

Polynesian traditions aside, the fundamental problem with surfing will always be how powerfully it drives the ego. There is nothing inherently social in surfing's purest moments, because riding a wave is 100 percent personal. It is all about your preparation, experience, timing, strength and agility. There is nothing "team" about it. So cooperation and humility takes a back seat to aggression and arrogance. Left unchecked, it gets to the point that we dare think of ourselves as masters of the waves after a good ride, and we usually paddle back out as fast as we can for another one. As long as you don't have to deal with other surfers and their egos and craving for waves, getting one good ride after another puts a surfer on top of the world.

But as with every powerful experience that involves self-inflation among individuals in a crowd, surfing can go from the sublime to the ridiculous in an instant, from euphoria and elation to fear and survival, from a generous free natural environment to a monstrous example of human greed and enmity. Surfers are the blessed sons and daughters of Kahuna gliding through Neptune's kingdom, until they start acting like troops of baboons defending territory against outsiders while engaged in internecine conflicts typical of lower-order primate communities.

Another apt comparison would be to the behaviour of the sea's most instinctually-violent species, predatory sharks. My first experience with a real local, not some land owner or unemployed carpenter or out-of-shape big mouth, was at Lennox Head in Australia, part of the territory of a 15-foot tiger shark. An apex predator, it feared nothing, and we got out of the water pretty quick the times he was spotted feeding on the larger fish in the area. Sharks are a highly territorial species, in contrast to another apex predator, the broadbill swordfish, well-known for its transoceanic migratory routes. Both species developed two hundred million years ago, and have remained essentially unchanged for the past fifty million years. But while the swordfish is an inspiration for speed and agility, the shark conjures visions of merciless pain and death.

So when you consider that some of the worst "surf rage" occurs in some of the world's best waves, it seems that surfing often oscillates between the wondrous hydrodynamics of the swordfish and the brutal turf tactics of the shark. One minute you're flying over the water in a perfect natural setting, only to have the waves turn into the vicious streets of South-Central LA. As Ice-T said, "Wear a wrong-coloured rag, go home in a body bag."

Now, surfing is as far from the inner city as you can get. Yet having a coloured wetsuit or board that IDs you as an outsider can make for real problems at some surf spots. This is truly absurd. At least in the 'hood there's a reason for the violence: unemployment, fatherless families, poverty, hopelessness. What reason do surfers have to throw down? Surfers are as blessed as any people on earth, and so it is particularly tragic when their egos are controlled by the corrosive evils of selfishness, greed and jealousy.

I don't know if there is another sport/art/lifestyle on the planet that offers as phenomenal an experience as riding a wave and yet is cursed with human behaviour in a classification with sharks and gangbangers. Surfing is an amazing thing to do, but seen through the prism of localism, it comes off looking pretty lame.

Look at surfing as a sport, and consider what it would be like if tennis was similar to surfing. You and I could be beginners just starting to volley when two hot-shot pros could show up and simply muscle us off a public court with taunts and threats while aiming powerful serves at us until we leave. Seen as an art, surfing fares no better. Surfers with bad attitudes are like graffiti vandals with overloaded minds aggressively chasing their fix of identity and recognition. In both versions, the surfing lifestyle is twisted into a joy-less, anxiety-driven fear of outsiders. Based on numerous personal experiences, that's what I've seen happen on the beach and in the water time and again.

My first confrontation with die-hard locals came at Topanga in the late '60s. I worked for Natural Progression in Santa Monica, and since they all rode our boards, they had to tolerate me. But I still got the "Out! Out!" when they saw me walking up the beach. I ignored the warning and got away with it. But when it came to unknown trespassers who didn't pay attention, the warning was followed by rocks and taunts and more rocks. And if an intruder ruined the wave of a local, things got really ugly. Of course, the boys' excuse was that they were defending a good wave from hordes of LA and Valley surfers. But in the end the Topanga locals lost, since all their houses were torn down to make way for a public parking lot and lifeguard station.

The Ranch was a similar situation. Being a boater or a guest, my tenuous connections smoothed the waters to a certain extent. Although the vibe was still in the air, it did not ruin the place for me. Not so for some friends of mine, including Angie Reno, one of surfing's great talents, who in 1971 had to fend off a machete attack from Jeff Kruthers, long-time Ranch local who now, ironically, sells Ranch parcels. So I guess if you have the cash, you're in. Sometimes. When I was up there just last year with Rick Vogel and Yvon Chouinard, both parcel owners who have surfed the Ranch for decades, we couldn't surf Rights and Lefts. Seems that given who was out at R&Ls that day, showing up with even one guest was verboten. Yvon put it bluntly, "I don't want my tyres flattened again." So we had to settle for surfing in thick kelp at an empty spot a mile away.

The Ranch brand of localism continues to be defined by wealthy owners and their doberman surf bros. This is in contrast to Oxnard, a working-class town with poverty-driven gang problems and high unemployment. As opposed to the privileged sniffiness of Ranch mossbacks, the worst locals at Silver Strand were usually unemployed construction workers or cholos who didn't even surf. In fact, we quickly learned that surfers in the water were often the least of our problems.

Today it is nowhere near as bad as when we wrote the book on surfing the place by avoiding locals who jacked up the unsuspecting and the innocent. Being "southers" from Santa Monica, we'd park on side streets and chat up residents into watching our cars. In fact, we pioneered the peaks in the middle of the beach because the north jetty parking lot was just too risky. Unfortunately, former Malibu great George Szigeti learned that lesson the hard way. After a great session, he got out of the water only to find four slashed tyres and every window of his new VW bus smashed – and a group of thugs waiting for him! So we had to be alert, and although we still had to deal with some real losers, when the waves got big we'd have the place to ourselves.

The Ranch and Oxnard have earned bad reps for localism, but Hazard Canyon, in central California's Montana De Oro State Park, was during the late '80s the worst cesspool of selfishness I ever experienced. Best on cold winter mornings with freezing winds whistling down the canyon, the place is hostile to begin with. With a small take-off zone and a thick, peeling barrel that made drop-ins extremely dangerous, the prevailing atmosphere was intimidating and tense. And since Park authorities were usually miles away, the Canyon was a setup that really stacked the deck against visitors. The regulars were no-nonsense tough-guys who could surf the place so well that you wouldn't dare look at a wave they wanted. But even if a local couldn't surf that well, he would still be a factor thanks to his longevity at the place, thick arms from pounding nails, or just plain shitty attitude driven by his own personal failings.

Led by Whitey and JG, it was a crew that revelled in its reputation for being violent assholes. Bradley Jordan, the best surfer ever to ride the place, took five years and several fights to break into the line-up. I lucked out: I knew Bradley when he was a grommet hanging around the NP shop in the Santa Monica days, so I gained entry through him. No-one ever got in my face, although what I saw and heard directed at innocent strangers made me cringe more than once in the three years I surfed the place.

As it turns out, I went back a few years ago, and things had changed to a certain extent. Whitey was still whining, the take-off zone was tight with carpenters and roofers with attitude to spare and the waves were merciless if you made a mistake. Yet the threat of violence did not hang heavy in the air, as if the crew had finally wised up a little bit.

But unfortunately, the primal instinct of localism rarely goes away on its own. Consider the Rockside boys of Port Hueneme. Their surfing traditions came from a tainted gene pool where localism was handed down from a generation of has-been long boarders to young high school dropouts turned wanna-be surf stars. These guys were real jerks – until one of their homies was convicted on assault charges when he attacked a teacher from Santa Monica surfing an empty peak west of the pier. The guy got probation that prevented him from surfing the place for three years. But, genius that he was, he was right back in the water a few weeks later, only to have a cop pull up as he was getting out of the water and take him straight to jail to do his time for the assault and violating probation. It was poetic justice that a Rockside rockhead did time for being not only violent, but stupid, too.

The fact that a surfer was put behind bars for being violent says that the worst of the localism as I've known it is on the retreat. One reason that things are changing is California Penal Code sections 243 and 245 dealing with aggravated assault. Victims are now calling the police, and in recent years the law has stepped in to protect the innocent and charge the guilty. Witness what happened in Palos Verdes or the assault in San Diego two years ago. Guys got arrested and convicted, and newcomers were able to surf without threats from mossbacks giving 'em stink-eye and worse.

Another reason that "surf rage" is abating somewhat is the fact that yesterday's surf hoodlums have grown up and now have kids, and if there's one thing that's going to change the life of an OG (LA slang for "original gangster"), it is having to be a father. A third reason for localism's overall decline is that, over the past five years or so, dilution has been the solution to the pollution of localism. There are now so many surfers everywhere that, as when Topanga was turned into a public beach, who is or isn't a local is now a moot point. Like King Canute ordering the tide to stop, the hard-core locals of yesterday are being swept into submission by a constant tide of recreational surfers spreading around the world.

This is good news. Surf spots are extra-special natural environments because they give people a chance to play with the ocean's energy. There is no cause for selfish and sometimes violent behaviour over waves that belong to no-one. As the legendary North Shore surfer Owl Chapman once said, "Be nice, share a wave, give a smile, say Hi." I couldn't agree more: a friendly vibe in the water makes the surfing experience complete.

Riding a wave is a perfect opportunity to test our human nature, face up to our failings and focus on bringing out the best in ourselves. Consider the non-violent example of Gandhi. He understood the devastating effects of an unchecked ego. For ten years he resisted becoming the leader of India's independence movement until he felt ready to be a powerful, yet selfless, man of inner peace. His autobiography, *The Story of My Experiments with Truth*, is a wonderful inspiration in dealing with the subjugation of ego.

So the next time you're tempted to vibe someone you don't know or take more waves than you deserve, consider things from the other guy's point of view. Only when courtesy and sharing define our behaviour is it possible to fully realise the promise of surfing. Show some respect for Mother Ocean and leave your ego on the beach. If you're a visitor, the same rule applies: don't be confrontational, but, at the same time, remember that you owe the ocean a lot, so don't turn tail and retreat without trying to work things out verbally. Localism is a toxic spill that has contaminated a lot of surf spots, and sometimes you have to help in the clean-up.

If you really have surfing in your heart and soul, you simply have to act in the name of civility in the water, starting with an attitude of cooperation and sharing. If it's too crowded, get out of the water and wait on the beach, or surf someplace else. Battling the pack endlessly brings out the worst in people. Same goes for any territorial feelings you might have about your favorite surf spots. There is no excuse for desiring euphoria so much that violence becomes a way to get it. This aspect of surfing simply has to change, and that's all there is to it.

As Charles William Maynes recently said with reference to Bosnia and Kosovo, "society ... depends on deference, deference to tradition, authority, to law, to treaty commitments. If you lose that, the only thing you've got left ... is force." In surfing, we have no governing authority, and the times we've resorted to criminal law to resolve our disputes have been excruciating embarrassments to the sport as a whole. So we must defer to each other in the water and respect the best traditions of riding waves: the travelling, the welcoming of visitors, and the sharing of waves exemplified by the early long boarders. Thus, we must commit to personal treaties of peace with all our fellow surfers if any of us is to truly deserve the joy to be found in surfing.

Yelling to get waves, challenging guys to fights on the beach, pushing off shoulder-hoppers, giving strangers stink-eye, dropping in on kooks: Lord knows I've seen and done my share. But let me tell you from personal experience: a surfer's soul feels much better when you really make a pacifist attitude a part of your surfing identity. Always being generous and cooperative, especially when the waves are good, can be a long and difficult lesson to learn: ask Johnny-Boy. But if we all behave as if our children are watching us surf, we will someday cleanse the stain from surfing's soul, and the localism and violence of modern surfing will be nothing more than a sad chapter in a distant past. I may not see it, but if there's anything I can do about it, my children will.

LOCALISM IN HAWAII

from a Haole Wahine* perspective.

Carol Anne Philips

Carol Anne Philips is a professional body boarder; the 34-year-old was born and raised within a stone's throw of Hawaii's famous Pipeline. She was twice Women's World Champion and numerous times Hawaiian State Champion before taking on the task of organising women's body board contests and going back to school. After 20 years of surfing every possible break in a line-up dominated by men, she has a unique perspective on the pecking order of the North Shore.

In 1893, Queen Liliokalani, a great defender of her Hawaiian culture, reluctantly turned her nation over to the United States government. The Queen did this to save Hawaiian lives. Although Hawaii is now regarded as just another American state, in fact its annexation in 1898 was passed only by a simple Congressional majority, whereas it takes a two-thirds majority to pass legislation that affects a foreign nation. I will leave it up to you to do the maths on the legality of Hawaii's current status:

Under international law when you have a violation of treaties of this magnitude, the World Court has ruled that the only appropriate remedy is restitution. Damages are not enough, reparations are not enough – that is, the payment of money – or giving you an island over here and saying, "Here, you can have that island". No, restitution, to restore what you once had, that is the Kingdom of Hawaii, your independent nation state, this is the appropriate remedy ... for what was done.

Prof. Francis A. Boyle, 28 December 1993

* A Caucasian girl raised in Hawaii.

I tell you all this to help put into perspective what has fuelled the anti-foreigner sentiment that is sometimes found in Hawaii. Unfortunately, the history of the Islands has been exploited by some to manipulate a territorial attitude that has, in some cases, extended into surfing.

Haole Wahine

I came to Hawaii from Califonia with my mother, twin sister and brother in 1970, when I was three years old. Someone gave my mum a one-way ticket to cook for a Peace Symposium in Waikiki. Needless to say, she fell in love with the beauty of the Islands and stayed.

The life I led growing up was unique – idyllic, some would say – and I do feel blessed. I was home-schooled and lived with my family at the end of a valley on the east side of Oahu. We lived a simple life, close to the land. Outdoor plumbing, cold water, and candlelight were the rule, and because I was home-schooled I was not exposed to the anti-haole (white person) prejudice that most white children educated in Hawaii have to deal with.

I trained in martial arts with my step-dad for many years; I learned the values of respect, discipline and self-control. The result was an open-minded, skinny local girl with long blonde hair, who was not afraid of other people.

I started bodyboarding when I was 17 and instantly became a surfer girl inside and out. I was living on the North Shore at the time, working the ponies at the Mokuleia polo fields, when I was kind of drafted into the sport at Pipeline. I lived across the highway, at the foot of the mountain, next to a fighting cock farm, and I could see Backdoor from my bedroom window.

Being a free spirit with the benefits of those years of martial arts training, and with a half-blooded Hawaiian bodyboarding champion as a teacher, I was able to paddle out and catch some pretty big waves right away. I remember landing on famed Hawaiian bodysurfer Mark Cunningham's head with a loud *thunk* on one of my first waves. He laughed when I asked him if he had felt it and said, "Yeah, didn't you hear it?"

Back then, no other girls rode the Pipeline, and the guys were extremely kind and considerate of me. On one of my first waves after I had figured out how to do a bottom turn, I accidentally dropped in on Johnny-Boy Gomes. He was getting ready to go ballistic and rip the wave to pieces, but – lo and behold! – who drops in on the shoulder but a haole girl, thrilled out of her mind to be going down the line for the first time – and, I should say, completely oblivious to the fact that she had just dropped in on one of the greatest surfers in the world (and oblivious to the "importance" of the Pipeline, for that matter). Johnny-Boy never said a word to me that day. But I think he spoke with my teacher, who then suggested that we paddle in.

The next time I was at the Pipe by myself, JB told me, "Go home." I agreed, then looked around, realising that I was home already. I continued my session.

As I said earlier, there were no girls out at the Pipeline when I started. But by my second winter, two other female spongers had been added to the line-up: France Hazar and Andrea Ferrari. They were, of course, Brazilians. Seeing France and Andrea in the water for the first time at the Pipe was a shock for me. I guess I didn't think of myself as a female – just a person. Well, with their skimpy Brazilian bikinis, these two were definitely female!

After that, more and more girls came from Brazil each winter, and soon female surfers from Japan and other countries started coming too. So in 1990 when we organised and competed in the first-ever women's contest at the Pipeline, we had a good field of talent, especially for a sport that had only ever had two international competitions before.

In Hawaii, I took a lot of flak for spearheading this event. However, I love the sport and, while I recognise the importance of what country issues you with a passport, I feel my strongest identification with other girls who bodyboard, no matter what their background. From a more socially-responsible perspective, considering the history of women's participation in sports and men's intense dislike of cellulite-ridden thighs, standing my ground was the only moral thing to do.

The event went smoothly for many years, growing until I was able to offer $US20,000 in prize money, with the generous sponsorship of G-Shock/Casio, and got some insane wave conditions. We got tons of press, and Ken Bradshaw pointed out that the girls had the best 10-day holding period of the winter; according to his records, year in, year out, we had the most consistent days for west swells. All of this helped inspire an ongoing campaign to take the event out from my control or even to stop it entirely.

So far, I am still running the event at the Pipeline and surfing every day the waves are breaking.

Hawaiian Attitude

I do not believe that Hawaiians are violent by nature; from my experience, they are quite the opposite. In an anthropological report entitled "The Surfing Community: Contrasting Values between the Local and California Surfers in Hawaii: Social Process in Hawaii, 1959", published jointly by Romanzo Adams Social Research Laboratory and the Sociology Club of the University of Hawaii, the historian Ben Finney compared the fundamental values of Hawaiian and California surfers.

Basically, Finney said that Californians tended to view surfing as more than a mere sport or recreation, and that all other activities in life were subordinate to it. Hawaiians, on the other hand, saw surfing as simply part of one's life. Just as one must work to pay the rent or catch fish to eat, one caught waves to have fun – it was just a part of life.

I believe that this was due in part to the fact that surfing was relatively new in the rest of the world. I recall that, in the beginning, I was totally obsessed with riding waves. I completely abandoned my family and social life, and bodyboarding became my only priority. I also had a feeling of superiority over the mere mortals on the land, as well as the small-wave riders in the rest of the world.

However, as time went on, I realised that the waves would always be there and that other parts of life were equally valuable. I went back to college and revived my relationships with my family and friends.

In my 20 years of surfing in Hawaii, I have seen very little violence.

This is the major difference between the Hawaiian perspective on surfing and the competitive and often violent nature of surfing today. The Hawaiians have been surfing for hundreds or maybe thousands of years. They know that the surf will always be there. Other cultures don't seem to have such maturity. Having only relatively recently discovered such a wonderful activity, they seem to value it over most other things.

The Hawaiian attitude is well described in this quote from a Hawaiian surfer: "We don't paddle our arms off to catch a wave like the 'Coast Haoles'. We try to catch the wave in the steep (curl), where it only takes one or two strokes to start the slide. If a wave requires too much paddling to catch it, we wait for another, steeper one" (from *Hawaiian Surfer*, by Ben Finney, 1959).

Surfing is a cultural activity that has been in place for a very long time as a part of a relaxed island lifestyle. Now it has been embraced by people from over 40 countries around the world. Life being competitive (and competition often leading to violence), this growth has naturally helped to shape the evolution of modern surfing culture.

When you have people coming from all over the world to the close-knit community of the North Shore on Oahu, with the sole intention of proving that they are the best surfers in the world, the locals tend to view this mentality with contempt. From the Hawaiian perspective, it takes a lifetime of dealing with the ocean to prove yourself, not only as a surfer but as a waterperson – not just one winter of catching the biggest waves or winning a contest at the Pipeline.

I think it's hard for locals in Hawaii to respect someone who comes here to try and show them up. There is also a type of brotherhood when the surf gets big: it's kind of like a club, and the only way to get admitted is to paddle out and take off. So, when a foreigner shows up and tries to prove that he or she is better then the members of the club – who have proven themselves over previous winters – it's like, "Please, dude, give it up and put in some dues first."

Newcomers will often try to outpaddle a local hero who has priority just by paddling for a wave. I remember one time when a Brazilian guy, who owned some wetsuit company, took off behind Gerry Lopez at Pipeline. I thought it was so rude of him – after all, Gerry is a household name in the Islands and the King of Pipe. Who would ever even think of hassling him for waves?

But for this guy it was, like, "I'm so good I can take

off deeper then Lopez" (even though his board was twice as long as Gerry's). Suffice to say, he didn't last long at the Pipe – or even catch any more waves that day. Some people have no respect.

Surfing-related Violence
From my observations, in Hawaii this most commonly stems from these causes:

- **egomania** – there are many people who consider themselves to be superior because of their physical build or (imagined) surfing ability;
- **hurt pride** from realising they are not the superior surfers they imagined themselves to be after having been bested by physically-smaller people; frustration arising from a lack of surfing ability or from some turmoil they have experienced on land and couldn't leave behind when they went surfing – or both;
- **territoriality** by people of mixed (non-Hawaiian) racial descent (those with a large percentage of Portuguese blood seem the most likely to attack others – a simple fact I have repeatedly observed over 22 years) and Hawaiian wanna-bes who like to try to show they are "local" and believe this gives them some kind of special right over others to ownership of the water. Apparently, on the outer islands, territorial aggression is even worse; as a kid, I heard rumours about a Hawaiian King named Titus (Kinemaka), who would eat haoles for lunch; and
- **greed** – the hunger to get as many waves as possible by any means possible with a complete lack of respect and/or regard for anyone else.

Conflicts erupt when large numbers of greedy people, lacking any social graces, compete for limited resources (waves) at the given time.

In general, violence permeates "local" Hawaiian society; it's endemic as a method of teaching discipline to children. Child abuse and spouse abuse are rampant. Only in the last ten years has this become a public issue, with real efforts being made in dealing with it.

Old habits are hard to stop and this mentality is bound to spill over into violence in the water when it is combined with any or all of the above ingredients.

Ugly Localism

The most horrific instance of localism in modern times came from the owner of a big Hawaiian surfwear company, who was offering $US25 per head for every Brazilian who was punched out on the North Shore.

I remember my Brazilian friend, France Hazar (who, being female, was not threatened by this bounty), being very upset and doing everything she could to protect her countrymen. I'm not sure how it all ended, but a lot of Brazilians were renting a house at Rocky Point from a Mrs Keawe and the rumour was that the landlady and her rather large Hawaiian family were not happy with the situation and pulled the surf-wear punk up smartly.

This guy really did not like Brazilians and one day he was parked at the end of the public right of way, checking the surf at Rocky Point, when some Brazilian-looking guys pulled in and parked behind him.

When he is ready to leave, the surfwear punk tells the guys, "Hey, move your car!" The "Brazilians" say, "Sure, just a minute", and they're checking the surf too. So the local snaps at them again, "Move your car now!" And the guys again say, "In a minute", so the local goes to punch one of them and gets a roundhouse kick in the head.

It turned out that the guys were from Israel and their family was familiar with the local's parents. He was a tad embarrassed, to say the least, and threw a luau for them by way of an apology.

In another instance, a famous big-wave surfer was riding Sunset years ago and missed a wave when choppy conditions hindered his ability to get into it. He began yelling the F-word at the top of his lungs and proceeded to punch himself in the head for 30 seconds, until a 12-foot set mowed him down. In an unrelated incident the same surfer was reported to have actually taken a bite out of another surfer's board as punishment for dropping in on his wave.

In the mid-'70s, on a perfect six-foot day at Laniakea, a local heavy (who will remain nameless) dropped in on a haole guy, causing the haole to wipe out. Somehow the haole's board hits our hero in the leg, and the local ends up between the guy and his board. As the haole begs for his board back, the local proceeds to tear the fin off with one hand, throws it at the guy, then swims over and grabs him by the hair and dunks him under water about 30 times. He didn't kill the haole, who was able to swim in on his own, but he was pretty pulverised. He was never again seen at Laniakea.

Another incident in the '70s involved Australian Ian Cairns at Ehukai Beach Park. Everybody knew that Ian was going to get his ass kicked over something he had said in a surfing magazine interview during the heyday of the "Bronzed Aussies" (Cairns' Australian surfing team).

A heavy local hired this big guy named Alvin to do the job. Apparently Ian was tipped off at the last minute to the large local aggressor hiding in the bushes near the lifeguard tower and a hilarious neighbourhood chase scene ensued. Somehow, the Aussie managed to outrun the moke, and Cairns was seen later that day, unscathed, surfing the rights at nearby Rocky Point.

On another occasion, Cairns was not so lucky, as he and his countryman, Wayne "Rabbit" Bartholomew, were attacked and beaten in separate incidents in the Sunset Beach area of the North Shore.

This was a period that saw the "Australian Invasion" of the North Shore; it got so bad that the Aussies had to hire personal bodyguards to surf in the contests, and they confined their free surfing to out-of-the-way spots.

About this time, witnesses saw fellow Bronzed Aussie and 1976 World Champ Peter Townend running from Sunset Beach to the Kuilima Hotel, carrying a pink surfboard, with 20 big locals chasing him. Suffice to say, the pink board was seldom seen after that.

Then there is the story of this crazy haole guy who used to surf at Haleiwa in the mid-'70s. One day, for no apparent reason, he started a fight with one of the locals and was seen chasing him up and down the beach with a sledgehammer, much to the delight of the beach crowd. After this, the haole apparently gave up surfing.

My final story concerns another famous surfer who has the distinction of being the only male surfer I have ever seen or heard striking a girl surfer. This drama unfolded just like so many other accounts of "surf rage", on a completely-normal, extremely-crowded, perfect day at Ehukai's sandbar rights. Another talented pro, Bud Llamas, dropped in on this other surfer (who will remain nameless), and, out of frustration, our friend kicked his board at Bud, narrowly missing his head.

The incident was witnessed by several dozen surfers in the crowded line-up, including the female Australian surfing star Jodie Cooper, who commented to our friend about the inappropriateness of his behaviour. In response, he gave her a quick backhand to the side of the head and was heard to say, "You wanna talk like a man, you had better fight like a man." This incident left everyone in the line-up shaking their heads in disbelief.

But then again, it all comes around. When this same guy beat up another surfer up at Sunset over some *manini* (small) incident, a week later the victim's Samoan friends came to pay our friend a call with a two-by-four; somehow he escaped with his life and went on to terrorise more surfers. He is currently on probation for aggravated assault charges stemming from another surf-related incident, this time at Chuns Reef...

IMPORTED SURF RAGE

Even paradise can be muddied when localism emerges.

Craig Jarvis

Craig Jarvis is a 30-year-old South African who has been travelling the world writing stories for surf magazines for the past 7 years. In 1994 while visiting Australia he came second in a SURFING LIFE writing competition and decided to have a go at writing on a more permanent basis. With all his travelling to remote locations in the past few years he is more than qualified to write on the spread of Surf Rage in his part of the world.

Travelling surfers consider themselves ambassadors with a vision of purity. They believe that they forge intercultural friendships, inspire humanity with their passion for life and dedication towards the wonderful places they travel to and the special yet simple people they interact with.

When they leave a pristine area they believe that they leave nothing behind but footprints and memories. But what really happens when surfing turns up on the doorstep of an unaffected third-world shore?

Here are a few examples.

Indonesia

When Kevin Lovett read the April 1974 issue of *Surfer* magazine, it was the images from an article called "The Forgotten Island of Santosha" that convinced him to head off on a voyage of discovery. The article, penned by Larry Yates about the Indian Ocean island of Mauritius, conjured up in Kevin's mind consistent visions of swaying palm trees and perfect surf, and these thoughts never deserted him while on his mission.

Despite the author throwing a red herring across the trail to the site of his experience by describing "Santosha" as not really a place, but a state of mind –

"actually a forgotten state of mind" – Lovett discovered another paradise, one of the great wonders of the surfing world, Lagundri Bay in Nias. The ultimate Elysium. A perfect right-hand barrel in warm water, no other surfers for thousands of miles, and friendly people living on the beach. "It was late afternoon, and the rich, equatorial tones in the sky cast an ethereal appearance over the bay. We stood on the point marvelling at both the magnificence of the wave, and also the incredible beauty of the backdrop which featured lush green covered hills with a golden sandy beach, fringed by incredibly tall coconut trees front-lit by the sunset hues. Continuous sets kept marching in, and while the waves appeared demanding they also looked perfect. The search was over. We burnt offerings to Buddha to celebrate the joy of life. The Dream was for real."

Lovett's discovery truly reflects how the importing of western culture and standards can and do completely destroy the fantasy. I read Lovett's story and headed off to Nias in 1998. Spent my birthday there and the next day I get a six-foot swell as a present. I paddle out, squinting from the harsh sun. I start chatting to this older Aussie about the waves and last night's party. Suddenly there's a set wave and this big fella's paddling for it. I leave it to him, but unbelievably some runt with a shaved head turns on his inside and takes off whistling and shouting. The big fella fades him magnificently and the bald guy, a Brazilian, gets worked and snaps his leash. He retrieves his board and paddles out, and so ensues a tirade of broken-English abuse. The big fella just sits there with a faint smile on his face, and when the torrent slows down he says, "Okay mate, on the beach. C'mon, let's go." They clamber over the coral right in front of the big coffee shop. The Brazilian picks up a chunky piece of driftwood and smashes the Aussie over the back of the head. Cuts a huge gash above his right ear and it knocks the fella over. Some local Indonesians run over and hold back the Brazilian before he gets another chance to swing. We're shocked. In reality, a blow over the head by a solid piece of wood could kill a man. As witness, I could have seen a man killed over a wave.

Sports sociologist Jay Coakley describes these situations as a form of "positive deviance" and over-commitment to the "sport ethic". Having larger numbers in the water threatens competent surfers to conform to the "sport ethic" so they over-commit to compensate. In simple terms, they drop in and get aggressive.

But this shouldn't happen. Surfing isn't based on capitalistic values. It is based on the purity of love for the sport. A love that has been fighting for years for possession of my soul. The recurring dream is over for me. I leave Nias the next day, and haven't been back since.

Mauritius

Despite the Santosha piece in *Surfer* in 1974, the island paradise had been discovered long before, and a story had run in *Surfer* magazine in September 1966, called "Mauritius – Surfing Paradise", by Ian Harewood.

"They came into our beach bungalow and we shook hands in the French manner. They were some of the local surfers: Patrice Bernard and Serge Koenig and Rico and Percy Bathfield. Some of us spoke English, some spoke French, but we had no trouble conversing because we had a strong common trait: we were all surfers. As we enjoyed a few icy Mauritian beers before dinner, the locals told us about the history of the sport on the island; it had been introduced by Arnaud and Joel de Rosnay, the Biarritz brothers whose family owns a sugar cane plantation on Mauritius. We listened to surfing talk; about 15-foot waves breaking on coral reefs, beach breaks and other spots which the locals considered too dangerous. 'Would you like to use my weekend beach bungalow at Tamarin Bay during your stay?' asked Bernard Koenig. 'It is right in front of the best surfing break on the island.' Tony and I exchanged glances. Bernard didn't have to ask twice."

South African Tich Paul would have been fourteen years old when Ian Harewood went surfing in Mauritius. He is now forty-eight and has spent his life travelling to all the surf destinations around the world except South America and Australia. Recently he went on a surf trip with his wife to Mauritius.

"The guys who I came across were called the White Shorts. I had heard about them but never believed that they would exist, let alone come my way, but they did. I paddled out at One Eye. There are only really two waves in Mauritius, One Eye and Tamarin. It's a fairly small surfing community. I imagine most of the guys would have been around as it was a fairly good surf day, six-foot and pretty good conditions. Good lefts. Reasonable. Not world class but reasonable. There were eight other guys in the water. I arrived in the car park. I was driving a hired car and had a buddy with me.

"An Australian guy came up to us and asked for some sun block. Introduced himself as Nathan. By chance he had just come from Cape Town and he happened to know my son and we got talking and he paddled out. We were just on a surf check so we went back to get my board. When I arrived there, a local guy was waxing up and there was a little boat running the guys out to the reef so I asked the boat guy if I could grab a lift. He replied that it wouldn't be a problem. The local guy busy waxing up didn't converse with me at all.

"I jumped in the boat and went out to the break. When the guy dropped me off he said to me that I must go and ride the right. Thing is, the right ain't no wave in my estimation compared to the left that the other guys were on and that was where I was going to ride. In hindsight what he was saying to me was that I'd better ride the right 'cause I'll get beat up if I ride the left. So I went over to the left, but I did see this guy Nathan riding the right. So I went over to the left, and I kinda felt the vibe was a little uneasy, there were about eight guys in the water.

"And suddenly my memory came back to me about the White Shorts. None of them was actually dressed in white shorts as far as I'm aware, I can't remember. So I thought 'OK, I'll take it really cool, I'll just hang on the outside'. A set came through and after the set there were about three of us left. Then I saw another set of four or five waves, so I thought I'd let these guys go and just move into line. I reckoned that they would see that I wasn't going to be a threat. That wasn't my set up. As I paddled into the line up one guy just stopped and grabbed me by the leg and said, 'Where are you off to?' I replied that I would really like to catch one of these waves. In response he turned around to me and said, 'In Mauritius only Mauritians surf. Get that into your head.'

"They had all given up the set, so that I couldn't catch a wave. Then he started screaming and shouting at me. I said, 'Look, I just want to talk to you. I haven't said anything yet.' He just carried on screaming and shouting. By that stage the other four or so guys had paddled back after their waves. I tried to say, like, 'Listen, you guys have complete right to the place, and whatever you don't want, I'm prepared to take.'

"I was thinking that in time some sort of brother-hood would come of it and they would see that I'm not a total dork of the water. In fact, on ability in the water, I would have placed myself maybe third. There were two guys who were surfing far better than me and the rest were way behind me in the pack, but I wasn't going to use that as my in anyway.

"With that, four or five guys surrounded me and just told me to get the fuck out of here. So I said, 'Listen, I'm just going to take like one wave and I'm out of here. I'm not really looking for this.' One guy spat in my face, which obviously I was really upset about, and the other guy just started dunking me once again, like a forty-eight-year-old tennis ball.

"So I climbed back on my board and said, 'OK guys, that's it. I'm out of here. Just let me get a wave.' They responded by herding me into the channel. They told me to paddle out, as they didn't want me there. With that I paddled over to the right. I thought that it was all getting pretty heavy and spoke to this Aussie Nathan who had just encountered the same thing.

"We tried to surf the right but there were rips and it was no good. So I caught one wave. On going back in the same guy who gave us a lift on the way out arrived and we asked him for a lift in. He was obviously unaware of anything that had happened in the water. He was probably even unaware that I had gone to the left and Nathan had gone to the left and that the whole thing occurred. He put us back in the boat.

"When we were going back in the boat, back to the shore, we overtook one of the guys in the water who had left and was paddling back. So we stopped to give him a lift. The guy refused to get in the boat with us, either we got out the boat or, well, he would not get in the boat with us. They had a huge quarrel and we carried on to the beach in the boat. When we got to the beach the guy dropped us off and I apologised profusely for the inconvenience or whatever and he just went totally ballistic at me. This is the boat guy. He had now had a fall-out with his buddy because of us.

Eventually they had a minor fight on the beach about the fact that he had given me a lift. We just thought that it was time to get out of there, that it was all way too untidy for us.

"And that was the whole incident. I didn't catch a single wave. So I went across to Tamarin Bay but it was only like two feet and I caught a couple of waves there. I was on a surf holiday, I was with my wife, you know, she's a good travel companion. I went back the next day and there was surf again and it was about eight in the morning. It was about four to five feet and no-one out and I realised that I actually couldn't really go out. My car was here; it would be very obvious who was out there. If I was to get trapped out there the threat, you know, is just too high. So after that I didn't surf again. I surfed Tamarin the once and that was my week's surf holiday. I felt totally deprived.

"In retrospect I can fully understand localism but I don't understand total aggression. Inhumanitarianism. What ever you want to call it. It's just not on, you know. To me it's just completely shocking. I'm not against guys protecting their rights. There is a way of enforcing it, but not in that manner. I was just there to actually have some fun; I made it quite clear that that's what I was about. I wasn't going to hassle anyone. It was just the spare waves that I would have taken."

So surfing, which we introduced to one of many paradises, is now out of bounds to us. All the good things that were introduced to the country have been replaced by all the bad things, all the negativity that comes along with progress. Surfing this paradise is set to become as extinct as the Dodo. The joys of surfing together with friends and strangers, enjoying the beauty of our sport in one of God's gifts to surfers, has become, as in Larry Yates' article so many years ago, "A forgotten state of mind."

Africa

There was a clean, spinning right-hand barrel in the corner of the beach. Without realising it, I slowly drifted down towards it. There was quite a crew on it, hooking into some hell barrels. Cape Town 1984: I was fourteen years old. The spot was called Llandudno. It was the first year that Cape Town had hosted an ASP event, the Spur Steak Ranch Surfabout. The pros were around, hassling with the local guys for a few of the gems. I was fully out of my depth. I had been surfing for about two years and there was still a wild, wide-eyed feel to it every time I paddled out. To see the barrels was an absolute marvel, to see the pros rip was a new and indescribably exciting feeling. I just paddled around making sure that I didn't get in anybody's way, scared shitless as I was.

There was this one guy out there who was snagging all the waves. I heard later that he was called "Wildman". He was hassling and snaking but getting some filthy barrels. He obviously had the place wired like only locals can. A set came through and it was perfect. To my grommet eyes it looked massive, like a solid six foot and just looming. I just started paddling away, heading for the channel. So the Wildman paddles for the wave and a kneeboarder is lying in his way. The Wildman paddles straight into the kneeboarder and sort of hits him while paddling past him. Just a sideswipe, a paddle-swipe. The Wildman catches the wave and makes the drop but doesn't make the barrel, gets caught behind in this thick, throaty monster. He surfaces and roars something out to sea. He is pissed off properly.

He paddles out to the pack milling around on the smallish take-off spot. On the way out he looks at me and I stare him in the eye. He has the glazed, unseeing look of a maniac, someone tripping, someone whose mind is not like my child-like and naive virgin mind. I look away and my young sphincter flutters.

He paddles straight into the pack, sits on his board and milks this kneeboarder in the face with all his might. This is all happening just a few metres away from me. My heart stops. I'm a little kid, right. Witness to a few brawls at lunch-break at school. Never kissed a girl. Studious. Insular. Fuck, I still played the piano! Never seen two grown men fight except on television. In a ring.

There is a spurt of blood and mucus as this guy's nose just crumples under his blow and he falls off his board. He's lying in the water, holding his nose and holding onto his board.

His mate screams at the Wildman, "Wrong fuckin' guy! You just hit the wrong fuckin' guy!" He points to the beach where there is another kneeboarder removing his fins. "That's the guy, you fuckin' idiot."

The kneeboarder with the blood nose recovers remarkably, fuelled by adrenalin, and says, "C'mon, you fucker, to the beach!"

They head for the beach. Some guys stay in the water where the waves are quickly becoming less crowded. Some others, like me, head for the beach. It felt momentous. I had hitched to the beach by myself, had no mates around to discuss this frightening situation with. But I felt I had to go and watch. It was like I was going to learn something, something that my friends wouldn't know about. Like I was going to become more grown-up by watching. Straight up there are a few punches thrown and a bit of wrestling. The guy with the bleeding nose is fierce and his anger takes the Wildman by surprise. A woman and her young children are sent scattering as the two brawlers tumble all over the beach. The kneeboarder eventually gets the Wildman into a headlock with his face in the shallow water. As the waves come the Wildman's face is held under water until the wave runs back. He is spluttering and panicking and I'm just feeling sick. Witness to the realities of life, to the physical sickness and stupidity of violence, to the thick dull smash of hard fist on bone. I have a vision of evil, of a deep and dark place, of pain and anguish and screaming souls. The Wildman shouts for release, the knee-boarder releases him and pushes him away violently and I as witness feel like I've been hit in the stomach, and my arms are shaking with adrenalin and fear.

My blessed sport, my saviour, the only thing that has kept me different from all the kids forced under our old school National Party regime to play school sports like rugby and worship Jesus, is destroyed in front of me. I feel a part of something deep and dark. A loose association of outcasts.

My vision of surfing's beauty is transformed in a matter of minutes and in the views of the families on the beach who had witnessed the whole incident I feel like a pariah for having a surfboard, and walk away an ashamed and very inconsolable kid.

* * * * * * *

My dad was never a short-tempered guy. Bringing up three kids he was tolerant and kind to us. Both my parents in fact were pretty mild with regard to their tempers. So I don't know where I got my temper. Could be my red hair, or maybe a righteousness burst of male hormonal angst during the important years.

It could have been the hangover, although the waves were absolutely firing and that should have been enough to keep me relaxed. It was a beachbreak with perfect A-frame peaks coming through. Every wave a barrel, the sort of day when you get tubed so many times it feels like you've been getting tubed all your life. Washes away all the flat spells and windy days.

Everyone was getting barrelled off his or her nuts and I was getting my share. This school friend of mine paddles out to join me. He's one year younger than me and a full intellectual, but a good guy and a good surfer. He sits alongside me and we rant about how good the waves are. It's his second surf and he'd been watching and seeing so many barrels that he decided to come for some more before the conditions changed. I've been waiting for a while and he's just paddled out so by rights the next wave should be mine. A perfect right appears right in front of us but he's got the inside track and takes off. He pulls straight into the barrel. I watch spewing 'cause there's no more waves in the set.

He paddles out with a big grin on his face and I let it go and smile for him 'cause it was a gem of a wave and we talk some more. Next thing a perfect left appears and he's got the inside track. He's a mate of mine and I just assume that he's going to give it to me and I paddle for it. But no. He takes off and grabs his rail. Pulls straight in. Fuck! He paddles back out, laughing at the stoke of that barrel and completely innocently he paddles right up to me and sits on his board.

I hit him as hard as I can. Flat hand across his face. There's a sharp crack as I connect and everyone in the water looks at us. "That was my wave," I snarl and paddle off. My heart's racing but I'm filled with rage. I sit on my board and look back. He's upset. Looks like he's starting to cry. I mean, I don't think that I hurt him but I definitely was the aggressor and he seems so confused. He paddles in and the anger drains away from me leaving me feeling wretched with an empty heart. "Aaaah fuck," I think. "What have I done?" Some little kids from my suburb are watching me. Some are in awe, some are shocked. I hang my head. The waves are still coming through thick and fast but

I've lost my rhythm. Once again I get the shakes and go in. I've shattered my own dream of perfect days with perfect barrels.

France

After my grommet eat-sleep-shit surfing days I went AWOL from the coast for awhile. About one year to be more precise. I went working in London. Drinking too much, eating shitty food and going to parties. Putting on weight. Taking drugs. Meeting girls, being wild. I lost all contact with surfers and surfing. It seemed at the time like I had too many of my own worries just fighting for survival that I couldn't afford the time for surfing anymore. Until I finally had to get out of London.

An Australian I had been working with called Oggie dialled me in on Hossegor. I went off with my little tent, an old surfboard and wetsuit and heaps of expectations. They weren't far off. The summer of '95 was pretty good in Hossegor with the Le Penon banks firing for weeks on end.

While hanging on the edge of the car park in my tent, alongside all these people travelling in deluxe mobile homes and stuff, I was witness for the first time to a sort of brotherhood of surfers that I had never experienced before. Well, I had never really surfed away from home before and London was but an ugly blot in my non-surfing past. A family of travelling surfers started hanging out in the carpark together and then moved on to a campsite in the forest together. It was cool. There were Aussies, South Africans, Kiwis, English, French, Germans, Dutch, and Spanish all hanging out together. Before I knew it some Kiwis that I had befriended gave me their old van. The engine had blown but it was still an excellent place to sleep in. I found an old mattress and shoved it in the back, tied some nylon across the roof to hang my board from, got myself a candle and a steady supply of red wine and I had a home, and became a part of the family.

But this travelling thing was still new to me. To be away from friends and family and have to make new friends was a little difficult at first. After a while it all sort of fitted into place. There were good people in the forest. Snail and Carwyn, and Tom and Joe. Robbie Page popped in here and there, Sarge was there for a little while with Simsy, and even world champ Tom Curren paid us a visit. The boys in the forest were generally prone to partying till late at night and after a while I got off this program and started doing the early to bed early to rise thing. Paid off with many an early barrel during this time of good waves.

I got up early one morning and padded down the forest path to the righthander at Cazane, just to the left of the old German bunker, which was slowly, over the years apparently, sliding down the beach into the water. The bank looked good and I paddled out alone. The beach was deserted. I knew that it wouldn't be long before hordes of surfers and men-who-prefer-the-penetrative-treats-of-other-men arrived to do their thing on this little stretch of sand known as Gay Beach. I got out the back at dawn. The water had warmed up considerably.

I had been surfing consistently for about two months now and felt fairly fit. Before I arrived in France life had dealt me a couple of bad cards, but right then and there, among the golden waves, I felt good about my life for the first time in a long time.

I hooked into a little right-hander. It zippered down the bank and I raced it through. Just getting the feeling, getting the rhythm. While kicking out in the shallows I saw some more surfers appear over the sand dune from the Le Penon car park. There were five other guys running down the beach. I was a bit bummed but there were plenty of waves coming through in the four-to-five-foot region and I was in such a good mood that I indulgently reckoned that things would still be cool, that there was still about an hour or so before the real crew pulled in.

I paddled out to the back, vanity sending me out to catch another corker while these guys on the beach could watch. Maybe I'd get a barrel.

Before I knew it, five jabbering Spaniards surrounded me. A good wave came through and I paddled for it. It was mine; I had been waiting for it. But this little Spaniard started whistling and suddenly swung around on my inside. I took off and he took off and started whistling. I kicked out. A little bummed but still tolerant. The rest of the newcomers all got waves of the set and I was out of place. The next set came through and I was waiting for the first wave. Again a little Spaniard whistled and snaked me and took off. I was by now a bit pissed off. The second wave was taken by the next in line of their crew with scant regard for my position in the line-up.

"Fuck this!" I reckoned and dropped in on the guy. He started wailing and shouting behind me. The wave started hollowing out. There was a barrel section looming, a Spaniard shouting behind me and the guy from the first wave floundering around on the inside. I did what any self-respecting surfer would do; I pulled in and rode straight over the guy on the inside. I hit his board hard and came flying off. The guy I had dropped in on surfaced right next to the both of us. Our leashes were tangled, they were shouting at me in rage, and two of us had clean incisions on our board's rails. I started telling them to fuckin' relax and untie the leashes when the guy who I had dropped in on hit me from the side. A full roundhouse swing to the face.

I was knocked over into the shallows by the ferocity of it as well as the surprise. I struggled to my feet and grabbed my face. My hand came away awash with blood. They were still ranting at me and pointing to the beach. I went in, shocked. Two of them started coming and the rest of the guys were paddling in as well to see what all the fuss was about. I was standing on the beach, bleeding from an as-yet unknown wound to the face, and outnumbered five to one on an empty beach.

I ran, hating myself for my cowardice, angry at the absolute unfairness of the situation. Wishing immediately that I had family or old friends or the family doctor nearby, but all I had was a few new friends in a clearing in a forest. I ran all the way to the clearing, I don't know when they gave up the chase. When I got back I woke up Joe. Joe was an Englishman and we had gotten on pretty well the last few months. Out of groggy sleep he staggered and took a look. Said that the cut on my cheekbone didn't look too bad, grabbed his mate Simon and tore off down the forest to find the culprits.

In this space of time the Spaniards had left, the beach had started filling up, and it was over, leaving me frustrated with a burning face, and bitterly cursing the betrayal that life had once again led me into. After all the turpitude that life had been dishing me over the last year or two, it had taken a fairly long time for me to once again regain faith in the goodness of the human spirit. And I had, through living with good people in the forest.

In the space of one morning my work had regressed somewhat. Got me back into thinking that the inherence of human nature leads towards bad. That people have to work, consciously and diligently, to be good. And so my circle of violence is complete.

But at my age making a conscious decision to

remain calm at all times when surfing in crowded conditions or with pigs is easy. But what about when you actually aren't allowed to surf: what happens when capitalism imports from first to third world and excludes middle class first-world citizens? Stated simply: what happens when you traipse half way around the world and get confronted by a price tag out of your range restricting surf rights to perfect waves? I'll tell you: it makes the blood boil.

Tavarua

I've never been to Tavarua, an island in Fiji. Never been able to afford it. The stories that ooze from it have always been on the sketchy side, enough to make me have serious doubts as to whether it would ever be worth it. The resort's founders, Scott Funk and Dave Clark, have used ugly tactics of violence, implicit and explicit, to stop non-guests from surfing their breaks for sixteen years now. Intimidation here is what holds the key. And hey, it works. I, for one, don't want to get my head kicked in by a Fijian heavy. Ferals can't surf here, neither can locals without permission. It is a world where the surfing dream shouldn't exist.

Hot Fijian local surfer Matthew Light tried to surf Cloudbreak when there were only five other guys surfing. A Tavarua-owned boat with ten Fijians arrived to escort him out of the water. He was dragged onto their boat. One of the big guys was cool but another wanted to milk him. He grabbed the poor surfer's rashie and was about to deck him when another of the boatmen grabbed his arm and stopped the punch from landing. This guy lives in Fiji and can't surf in his own country!

The capitalistic values march on relentlessly. Violence and coercion are overlooked, as more people get pockets full of cash. Local villages clash. One of the world's finest waves is owned by a few wealthy

Californians, and all with the tacit approval of the world's surf magazines (except *Australia's Surfing Life*, which has long maintained an anti-Tavarua stance) and companies who send surfers and photographers there each year.

Besides the charge per surf, and the wave rights and the exorbitant costs and the official Fiji bodyguards who have assaulted guys who try and surf there via other means, there is a completely different phenomenon that I, as a travelling surfer, cannot get my head around: the guys, paying guests from anywhere in the world, who complain when other guys get into the line-up and set Fijian muscle to use force to stop these guys from surfing. The mind set that absolutely destroys everything that the tribe ever stood for. A form of warfare. Surfers using Fijian heavies as weapons to beat up other surfers and to keep them away from the perfect waves of Cloudbreak, by force and fear.

Where has it all gone? How can these guys call themselves members of the tribe?

Indonesia

And then there's my failed attempt to sell the dream. My third time to Bali. There had been a few changes. More buildings, more people. More noise, more dirty water on the streets and more vendors shouting their wares at me. As usual, there was less swell. Tiny waves at the beachbreaks and a few waves on the extreme south of the peninsula. I booked into a cheap room just off Poppies II and unpacked. Planned my week in this corner of paradise. Things didn't look too bad. I still had some cash, the Internet had predicted some swell and I had hooked up with the same taxi driver from my last visit two years ago. Also, there was this absolutely beautiful girl staying in a room across from me. She had a baby daughter with her but it appeared that they were travelling alone. She had blonde hair and an alluring body and seemed friendly enough. On the second day of my stay she came and swam with me in the pool in her light-blue one-piece costume. She was stunning.

It didn't take long for me to find out that she was from Amsterdam and she had a husband who was spending all his time surfing at the beachbreak. He was travelling with a lovely wife who looked after their cute little daughter and bought him beers in the evenings after he had surfed his brains out all day.

That night I met Frank.

He came walking to the hotel, sunburned and caked in sand and struggling with his massive long-board and my dislike was confirmed. What's the point in travelling around the world if you're going to end up surfing tiny Kuta Beach on a bloody longboard? I couldn't fathom it or warrant the waste of time and money. My emotional baggage towards barge-riders came flooding back but we greeted each other civilly. His wife smiled.

The next morning Made picked me up and I went off for an early morning surf at Ulus before the crowd arrived. As I was locking up my room Frank woke up, saw me leaving and waved goodbye. The waves were small but fun and uncrowded and I surfed for about four hours. Then the crowds arrived en masse and my surf was over for the day. I headed back for the hotel. Kuta Beach was about three feet but it didn't warrant a surf. She had been swimming with her daughter and was standing outside her room dripping wet. I was just placing my boards down outside my room. She calmly stripped off her light-blue one-piece costume and stood there completely naked before picking up her daughter and walking into her room. I was visibly shaken at first. Was this a come-on? Was it just a tease? Was public nudity common behaviour to people from Amsterdam?

I decided to befriend them.

* * * * * * *

Ulus is a tricky mission to negotiate. I mean, it's not that bad but the climb down can be difficult, the paddle out can be a bastard as well, and the local boys can be a bugger. On top of this the vendors can be pretty full on. For someone like me all these things are just commonplace, the minor irritations one has to negotiate in order to survive in a place like this. I really didn't even notice them until I realised that they were really freaking Frank and his wife out. But Frank was game. He had read and heard so much about Ulus that he was definitely going to surf it, no matter what. He negotiated the ladder down into the cave with extreme difficulty. There wasn't much I could do, as access to help is limited. I also believe in the school of thought that if you can't get your equipment down to the water's edge by yourself, you really shouldn't be in the water with it. He had his longboard nestled in the crook of his neck and was swaying off balance. I kind of hoped he would fall.

Accept that this was all a bit much for a longboarder from Amsterdam, but he managed to get down into the cave unscathed and my evil thoughts were gone. Next was the paddle out. Four-to-five-foot waves at low tide. Frank hobbled over the sharp coral. It took him an absolute age before he was in deep enough water to paddle, but once it was deep it was quick for him to get out. I paddled out alongside him, watching him negotiate the whitewater in various different ways: jumping off, eskimo rolls, bailing out.

Now I don't profess to know too much about Indo and its politics: apart from being shouted at at Bingin,

I've pretty much kept to myself. Stayed out of trouble. So we're paddling out and I'm kinda proud of getting Frank out at Ulus.

He's really excited. This guy from Amsterdam is in an alien world, he's on a journey to somewhere weird and exciting and I'm his link, his little safety-line. A set comes through. A little kid paddles for the first wave but Frank and I aren't quite clear and the boy has to pull back at the last minute to avoid us. Frank is oblivious to the little drama in front of us. He's a little scared of the set and of the coral bottom so he just keeps paddling, unfortunately in a beeline for this little bunch of kids. He gets in the way of a second guy and then the set is over. He sits on his board among these little kids and smiles at me with obvious relief. A burly, chocolate-skinned gentleman paddles over briskly on a board that is clearly underbuoyant for him. He looks like a bit of a fool.

Fists fly and Frank cops one in the mouth and one on the head. Gets a nasty-looking cut across the cheekbone. He goes flying off his longboard, much to the delight of the kids, who start jeering. He looks around obviously a little dazed. He catches my eyes, completely confused. I paddle over as fast as I can before this buffoon unleashes another one.

The ignoramus sees our connection, and tells me that the kids are practising for a grommet contest and would I fuck off and surf further up the point, and would the longboarder please fuck off completely and never come back to Ulus. I guess thirty years of being hassled by Aussies has been too much for this guy.

We go back to Kuta and head off to a very cool chemist on the main drag, a place I had been to with nasty coral cuts before. The proprietor is a mellow old dude and sorts Frank out. We talk about the incident and Frank is angry and hurt and starting to get a little animated. The proprietor doesn't understand what has happened. Doesn't understand the concept of fighting in the water. I really am at a loss to explain it to him. We leave with a new bottle of hydrogen peroxide. A few nights before I had spent the night drinking whiskey with Frank while his wife was asleep, telling him all about the dream. About how I travel around the world with no money and surf the most beautiful waves in the most exquisite places. How surfing can touch your heart and allow you to be young and free.

How, when all is fucking out around you, sometimes when you go surfing it all washes away. Makes sense. Clarifies. By the time we had finished the bottle and were starting on a few beers he was sold, in his drunken state, to the dream, to my idealism that if you follow surfing it will eventually look after you. If you stay true to what it stands for, and surf for the pureness of it, it will provide you with all you need to be happy, to find yourself, to self-actualise.

Modern man, however, all too often finds himself wallowing in bitter cesspools. Greed and the relentless hunt for more and more applause.

Surfing should provide everything. It should be the one thing that you can always turn back to when life takes on one of its meaningless personas and knocks you down.

Surfing should always save you.

And all that my dream had provided to this super-keen, over-age grommet from a non-surfing home was two stitches across his cheek and a fat lip. Greed leads to violence. Greed for money, or the selfishness for more waves. Yet greed can be kept in check. All a surfer has to do is look out at night from the bows of a feral Indo fishing boat to where the moon casts its silver coins along the shoreline. For there is a treasure that can never be spent.

TERROR IN THE SALTBUSH

The author enjoys the unique hospitality of Australia's heaviest locals.

DC Green

For half of his 35 years DC Green has jolted surf magazine readers (and editors) around the world with his biting satire, gonzo travel exploits and brutal vivisections of the ASP's contests. He normally attends two every year to replace his worn-out free contest T-shirts. DC's dubious writing credentials include creating Lash Clone, a cult character from planet Vortex who appeared in over 80 issues of TRACKS. He defeated Kelly Slater on a pool table in G-land and popularised the word gonad.

Every Australian beach evolves a unique communal hierarchy and philosophy, usually around a core of older, respected locals.

Perhaps the most infamous locals in Australia are those who surf in the desert region around the town of Saltbush*, in the Great Australian Bight.

The paranoid and violent locals of Saltbush don't take kindly to uppity strangers who want to expose the local waves: "Er, sorry, cunt. Didn't mean to smash ya camera!"

Saltbush was never a wise destination for a surf magazine promotional trip. But as a journalist who should have known better, that's exactly what I did: led three professional surfers and a photographer right into a showdown with Australia's heaviest locals. Was it worth the cost?

We were hurtling about 175 clicks an hour when one shock wave from an oncoming truck too many tore our surfboards from the roof for the third and final time.

---

* Saltbush: real place; wrong name.

With those boards flew whatever hope we had of reaching the City of Churches airport before gate closing. I jammed on the brakes and we began to slide. The heavier board-bags ploughed into low scrub or skidded hard straight down the highway, scattering cars like chickens.

The loose boards spun through the air, higher than telegraph poles. Enviable.

Dust consumed our smoking sedan. Five bodies stumbled out to stare back dumbly at the carnage.

I'm not sure who cracked first, but it possibly was me. As if seized by some vengeful demon, I leapt up on the bonnet, cackling as metal crumpled beneath my jumping. Higher! The others ripped into the Ford body with door kicks and double-fisted punches to the boot, eyes crazed with stomached rage. Smash! Harder!

Only when no panel remained unpunished did we as suddenly desist. In awkward silence we stood as one, wheezing and ashamed, like a wired Seppo platoon gone nuts for just a few seconds, but who in that lapse had blown away the people of a Vietnamese village who'd broken off from rice planting in the hope of handout Hersheys.

South Australia can do that to grown men.

Or, more specifically, Saltbush will do that to fool surf journalists.

Yes, I was the fool who ignored all sage advice and drove that infamous mission of pro surfers right into the Saltbush camping spleen and a near-fatal clash of cultures. Even more foolishly, I believed I possessed some vague historic connection protection because my big brother called me Saltbush before I was even born and took cover from conscription there in the early '70s. I suckled on tales from his generation about the big, cold walls where the desert slaps the sea and a brotherhood of surfers live in golden harmony.

Saltbush was Indonesia before Indonesia even existed for surfers: a mystical if dangerous land of waves, far, far away.

Ten-odd years on and Indonesia had well hooked my generation (and every other). Tales of Saltbush were sparser, and no longer quite so golden. Still, I almost made it there in '89, only to bail out of a surf trip at the last hour due to insufficient wallet thickness. The decision still haunts me. The two surfers who set off without me collided head-on with a loaded semi-trailer somewhere east of Broken Hill. In the drunken wake of a double funeral that rocked Ulladulla, I swore I'd work my way to Saltbush one day, and ride a good set each for CB and Greg.

That day looked unlikely for a while. I started a bloody business and almost forgot what surfing was. Until some five years on. Derek Rielly, the new editor in all but name of *Australia's Surfing Life*, was aching for a visual antidote to coverage of gaudy yet irrelevant contests and media junkets promoting exotic surf camp destinations via glossy pimp pages.

So Rielly began negotiating with the only journalist available (fool enough) to commit to a much more hard-core (cheap) surf project for the magazine: me. I was so desperate to escape 70-hour working weeks that I ignored the warning sirens and signed up for the first-ever Operation Tubequest.

Three different crews of young pro surfers would ride shifts with me and *ASL*'s best photographers in a turd-brown V8 purpose-bought to rumble from the West Oz border through South Oz, Victoria and up the South Coast of NSW.

Like world peace, Tubequest seemed a cool, workable concept at the time.

* * * * * * *

At least I had no gripes about the troops. Andrew Ferguson was the Black Occy in more ways than one: a power-packed Aboriginal goofy-footer from Coffs Harbour with the ability to rip spontaneous jaw-dropping moves and a ready laugh for any situation.

Jason Gava was the Carver: a solid power surfer who revelled in big, square stuff. An experienced campaigner, Garve became the Surfer Organisational Officer with a philosophical word for any situation.

"Ginger" Mick Campbell was the cheeky grommet. Today Mick may be a tightly-muscled and focused challenger for the world crown, possessing a somewhat twisted sense of humour, but in '94 he was a scrawny unknown with no challenger for the tailbone-shattering mid-back seat and a (less developed) twisted joke for any situation.

Tubequest's first-ever photographer was legend lensman Bill Alexander. A stocky bullshit-free zone from the Central Coast coal mines, Billy always busted out the right lens and camera for any situation (either that, or his surfboard). He'd also travelled the coast further around from Saltbush many times. Other South Oz locals respected him. At one fishing town, Bill had even struck up a de facto deal with the heavier locals: he wouldn't shoot their primo secret wave; in return, Bill's vehicle would not be smashed, and he would be allowed to shoot the less-impressive local waves.

* * * * * * *

From the outset, Tubequest threatened to become an unfunny joke. Preparations were abysmal – no-one brought enough money, we had a single two-man tent between five of us, while all Ferg brought along to ward off the sub-zero desert cold was a single green blanket. The thundering Tubequestmobile itself was a mechanical nightmare with a leaky boot, no heater, no stereo and no functioning speedo or fuel gauge (we only learnt this the hard way).

Besides needing the addition of Bill's trailer to fit all our gear, and regularly shedding boards from the roof like skin, the beast also endured three flat tyres, two snappings of the trailer couplings and the radiator water Biblically turning into liquid tar. The only car components that seemed to work were the vents that would mysteriously kick in at sundown, blasting icy air up everyone's legs (I ended up driving in my sleeping bag). The overburdened V8 also consumed half the GDP of Bangladesh in fuel, and more than our entire trip budget, just to even reach South Oz. There, despite consistent swell, we struggled to find photographic waves. It was either cloudy, or foggy, or the wind would swing onshore just as we arrived, or something else would drop out of the engine.

So, what to do?

"Let's go to Saltbush," I suggested.

The pro surfers had heard the horror Saltbush tales – like how a posse of psychopathic locals had ordered Rabbit Bartholomew and a crew of Billabong surfers to depart, or else, and how the vehicle of that same crew was sabotaged down the coast, causing the mission, and state, to be abandoned forever. In the three subsequent years, no surf media trip had gone anywhere near where we skulked now, let alone to Saltbush.

We'd been warned: "Some places have one or two crazed locals. But in Saltbush, they're all crazy."

So it was little wonder the Tubequesters looked at me as if I had begun frothing like a rabid dog, despite my best attempts to convince them that we would be making an honourable pilgrimage, that we would be respectful and win over the so-called crazed locals with the sheer integrity of our mission. In truth, a rabid dog would have frothed more sense.

"It might even be fun!" I beamed. "We're not plunderers. We want to meet the locals, to document their views!"

This made the troops mutter even less keenly.

So I changed tack. "Fuck the locals. We've got Ferg on our side. His people have been locals in this country for a thousand times longer than any of the so-called locals at Saltbush!"

Finally, the key hold-out relented, if just to shut me up. "We'll need firewood," Bill muttered grimly. "There's no trees at Saltbush and it's bloody cold." All right! So we drove, and drove. A few hundred clicks out of Saltbush we trekked into the last of the scrub and tied a few dead trees onto the board bags on the roof (which caused the roof to cave in).

We arrived at the camping ground around midnight. It was dark, the other campers were asleep and we were all too dazed at just being there to unstrap our trees and build a fire, let alone erect the silly tent. I found a hollow behind a saltbush to shelter from the desert wind, and snuggled in.

* * * * * * *

We climbed a dune, still stiff and stunned in the heatless sunshine. "No-one's tried to kill us yet," joked Mick, though of course no-one had figured out just yet exactly who we were. One car in the dusty park had number plates so rusty not a single digit could be read. But what cop would be crazed enough to venture out here to Mad Max territory to enforce a few defect violations? What surf trip would be silly enough?

The surf was clean, but small and crowded, so we set off to a semi-secret wave further around the coast. Bill navigated the maze of desert tracks, past signs with helpful warnings like "Trespassers will be shot. Survivors will be prosecuted". We arrived to find

Vortex cranking, with just four surfers out. One guy strolled over from a van, leaned in and muttered, "Look, I'm not a local. But you guys better not all paddle out at once." Bill already knew this unwritten crowd control law, but he thanked the guy all the same.

We decided to send Mick out first, the grommet being the most expendable. From land, we could hear the single local in the water screaming at the ginger to fuck off as soon as he paddled out.

When Bill set up his camera on the beach, the local really lost it. He steamed in, so I jogged down from the carpark to provide Bill with backup. I arrived to hear "Saltman" demanding that Bill pack up his camera, with colourful threats, implicit and explicit. Bill argued for a while, even let Saltman peer through his lens to see that the location could not be identified because of the tightness of the shot, but the guy would not be deterred.

"If any of the hierarchy turn up and see that I've let you take any photos, they'll throw rocks at me as well!" he almost pleaded.

So Bill relented and packed away his gear.

The surf pumped all day, crisp, sunny and offshore. When a few guys came in, we sent out a few more surfers. Saltman continued to argue with Bill and me all day, both in and out of the water. I showed him similar travel articles I had written that did not reveal the names of surf spots, and assured him that we only wanted to document surfing in the desert, not draw big maps.

Besides, I argued, if every area held the Saltbush attitude – zero tolerance to articles and photos – then we would live in a world devoid of surfing magazines, and probably still be riding 12-foot balsa boards. In fact, if there had been no magazine articles about Saltbush in the '60s and '70s, surely many of the incumbents would never have learnt about the waves in Saltbush in the first place. (Interestingly, early Saltbush articles raved about the natural beauty of the area in pseudo-spiritual hippie tones, all brotherhood and sharing: concepts that seem the very antithesis to today's blinkered "hierarchy".)

Saltman's response: "Even if you don't name names, cunts will still recognise a spot."

"But they'll only recognise this spot if they've already been here," I countered. "So it's no secret to them."

"But they'll all show their fuckin' mates the photos, and tell them where it is! Unless ..."

Saltman's face lit up with a brilliant notion.

"You could say any photos from here were taken somewhere else! Why not west Tasmania?"

Jesus, I thought.

"Because then all the west Tasmanians will be as pissed off as you are."

"Then say it's in fuckin' Namibia."

I tried to explain to Saltman, in my most diplomatic way, that most surfers already knew about the waves in the desert, but 99.9 per cent were unwilling to make the trip because of the vast distances and expense involved, the harshness of the land and lack of even basic facilities, the numerous Great White attacks, the near-complete absence of human females and the renowned hostility of the male locals. Why put up with all that when it was cheaper and easier just to fly to warm-water Indo?

Still, the arguments weren't all circular. Saltman and some guys from down the coast added to our stockpile of apocryphal Saltbush tales. Like the deranged locals who burnt down the only house ever built at Saltbush. Or the visiting surfers who had had cameras and windscreens smashed, even cars pushed off cliffs. One surfer told us how his car broke down on a Saltbush back-track. It took him a few hours to walk to the main track, toting an empty fuel tin, whereupon he was confronted by two locals who had been following him, one on a motorbike, both with guns.

"You're fuckin' lucky you stayed on the track, cunt," was all they snarled.

Another guy snapped his legrope on a big day. Half-drowned, he was washed onto the rocky shore, where he was met by a big local, the missing board under his arm. The local placed one foot on the half-drowned guy's head and sneered, "You can have your board back, cunt ... if you buy an ounce of mull off me."

Oops. There goes the m-word. Hard to avoid South Australia's biggest cash crop though, especially considering the role it plays at Saltbush. Guarding giant mull crops on forcefully-converted Crown land while consuming fifty-plus cones of stinking desert buds a day is hardly conducive to forming a rational, non-paranoid view of the outside world.

Saltman showed this aspect when I expressed an interest in talking to other Saltbush locals.

He quickly replied, "Oh no. No, no."

As if to a child, Saltman patiently explained that any local who collaborated with the media would be dealt hell forever by his mates. It just wasn't worth it. So I wondered, if this were true, how much like the surrounding saltbush the locals had become: low-slung, grizzled and indistinguishable from each other. They kept their heads down in order to survive, or else raised their fists in unison, in window-smashing mob rage, whenever they felt their turf was threatened. I wondered also what would happen to Saltman, when the extent of his dealing with us was outed.

Thankfully, the entire day was not spent in debate. As the sun marched higher, the crowd thinned, and we all ended up surfing our brains out. I felt sorry for Bill – here we had thumping swell, perfect conditions and three pro surfers absolutely blazing for the first time this trip and he couldn't take a single happy snap.

Salt in the wound: Bill's first session was a shocker, even worse than mine.

We rallied back to our campsite for a quick lunch of cold baked beans and black bananas. Ferg stayed behind to cook up a Ferg Surprise dinner and maybe get a few waves out the front, while the rest of us blasted back to Vortex: just in time to be met by another local, Sharkman.

Saltman had obviously informed this infamous shark attack survivor of our presence. No sooner had we stepped from the Tubiemobile, than Sharkman was shaping up to hit Bill and cursing, "This is our country! Ours!"

"Yeah, no photos!" added Mrs Sharkwoman from the Sharkman ute.

A weary Bill muttered back, "Look, I'm not taking any photos today. I just want to go surfing."

After a few more threats and rants, Sharkman's demeanour suddenly altered. He apologised for his behaviour and even told us we could shoot the main break at the Saltbush camping ground, before leaping in his ute and driving off. This swift direction change and apparent major concession left me feeling a little wary.

But I had more important things to worry about – like questing tubes! By the end of the day even the pros were surfed out, leaving just Bill and me in the water for a Team Media expression session that neither of us will ever forget. Bill redeemed his earlier shocker with some of the barrels of the day, on his backhand to boot. Even the fool journo scored a couple.

On shore, Saltman smiled, pleased that he'd halted the exposure of Vortex.

Having noted our vehicle make, model and colour, he farewelled Mick and Garve with a cheery invitation for us all to drop into the Saltbush pub to meet the other locals. When Bill and I finally came in (too dark to see) to hear this latest twist, my wary feeling grew like resurgent cancer.

By the time we returned to our campsite (via yet another flat tyre change), the sky was riddled with stars. We were all hungry and tired. Except Chef Fergie. Though his beans deluxe on the fire were somewhat overdone by now, they still smelt better than any beans we'd ever smelt.

So when I said, "Let's eat fast and get out of here," the communal response was, naturally, "Don't be so paranoid, DC."

Then we heard the engine. Engines. Jesus! Everything that all of us were and ever could be was thrown into sudden two-dimensional relief by the headlights bursting from the desert dark, bouncing up and down over the dunes, signalling what all of us feared most: a wild, honking, yee-haaing posse straight from the bowels of the Saltbush pub. It was Judgment Evening. And we would be the judged.

The other surfers at our fire quietly skulked off into the night. Old Holdens and rusty 4WDs pulled up all around us. Doors opened and crunched shut. A single voice echoed through the night air.

"Where's the cunts from *Surfing Life*?"

Sweet Jesus, I thought.

"I'm Bill Alexander," brave Bill piped up, "a surf photographer."

The posse leader zeroed straight in on Bill. He pushed him hard in the chest, causing Bill to stagger back.

"Calm down, mate," I croaked.

The leader spun. "And who the fuck are you ... cunt?"

"Ah ... I'm DC Green, a surf journalist."

The leader's eyes lit up as dark figures surrounded us and he ranted the now immortal line: "I don't care if you're DC Purple, cunt!" I knew then this was Fearman, the head crazy who'd confronted the Billabong crew, and ordered them to fuck off, cunts.

It was my turn to receive a vigorous push to the chest from Fearman, and a blast of liquor breath to the face. I was scared close to shitless, but I knew I couldn't let Fearman see that. I concentrated on matching his stare, on projecting confident body language to mask my quivering interior. Fearman was clearly keen to provoke a fight in the classic pub style, but Bill and I, who stood at opposite ends of the fire, kept him zig-zagging somehow, confused as to which of us deserved to be punished first, or the most.

Another guy stepped forward from the darkness, as if to calm Fearman. "I'm the Mediator," he spoke softly, and I thought, oh good, until the Mediator produced what seemed to be a stabbing weapon with brass knuckles, and waved it in my face.

Sweet, sweet Jesus.

"You cunts just want to exploit our waves," Fearman was snarling at Bill. "Just like you drag these grommets around by the nose!" Uh, oh: the divide and conquer technique at work. The pros remained squatting quietly around the fire. What else could they do? Run? Where?

"Why didn't they send Tim Baker?" demanded another voice from the dark.

Yeah, why didn't they?

"You cunts are lucky Elkman is in Indo!"

A tall guy – Beardman – lurched forward and cried at us, "We've got no water, no electricity, no nothing out here! All we've got are our waves ... and our mull."

He turned and yelled at his mates, "We don't know

these cunts from a bar of soap! How do we know we can trust them?"

And I knew then: they couldn't. After all, I was a journalist, an easterner, a media vagina introducing cameras and pros like smallpox to all these freaks held dear. Just as nineteenth century Oz feared the Yellow Peril sweeping down irresistibly, so we represented a potential vanguard of eastern yuppie hordes to these most insular of locals. If they let us go, would we boast that the Saltbush locals had turned soft? That would be even more terrible. So ... cut out our tongues? Nope, I could still type. Kill us? That seemed the only logical solution, especially if violence began, creating a need for a cover-up. So, kill us, and cover up our bones deep beneath the dunes. It would only take one of them (or us) to lose his cool, for the first fist to fly; the first knife or gun to be drawn. I figured Bill would probably stay on his feet the longest of us all, though once one of us went down bleeding, the rest of us would of course have to die as well, for dead media cunts tell no tales.

By now my mind was racing as fast as my heart. An emergency plan coagulated in my mind, a plan so desperate and unlikely to succeed, I almost laughed out loud (which would doubtless have brought forward the killings). Fearman was the most pumped up, and about my height. I figured as soon as the situation deteriorated another notch, I would approach him with my arms spread wide, as if beseeching peace, then bury my kneecap into his gonads with every terrorised drop of adrenalin I could muster.

My second target, assuming I was still alive after the first, was a pile of rocks near the fire. I would grab a fist-shaped one and go for the Mediator, as he was the one guy I knew for sure was carrying a weapon, plus he seemed probably the next most unstable after Fearman. I was secretly hoping Bill would take down the Mediator, though it was obviously difficult to communicate this desire.

After that, I would jump into the Tubiemobile and lock my door. Hopefully, my shaking hands would be able to fire up the beast before glass rained upon my face and I was dragged shrieking from the shattered Ford. If I could only get that far, I figured we'd have passed 50-50 odds. I would then charge the Tubie at the remaining locals, hopefully scattering them. Hopefully also, our guys would leap into the Tubie without any casualties. As for our boards, trailer and gear outside the car, I figured, fuck it all. With an angry posse on our tail, simplicity was the key: drive like a fuckin' madman, pray the V8 could stay ahead of the pack (and not run out of fuel), and zoom to the nearest town and police station, just a few hundred clicks away. It was a good plan, for a Big Arnie movie. But this was life, and possible death, up against a bunch of the orneriest, hardest-drinking, bred-to-it brawlers in the land.

Luckily, Saltman muttered a few words in our favour, while the general debate kept stalling on particulars. Bill simply would not surrender the film with the few shots he had snapped of Mick that day.

"Then we'll run over your fuckin' tent if you don't!" threatened Bigbeard. "Give 'em the film, Bill, give 'em the film", I telepathically pleaded, but Bill had his back up.

"No-one touches my camera gear! No-one!"

Eventually, thank Huey, Bill agreed to surrender the film if the safety of his equipment was guaranteed. When the ejected film was melting down next to our burnt dinner in the fire, the mood changed markedly. The locals began to laugh and relax a little, as if (brilliant) Bill's holding out for so long had only made their victory taste the sweeter.

Next things really got weird. Beardman grunted, "At least these cunts are doing it a bit hard core, sleeping out here rather than at the pub. Not like when Rabbit and them Billabong cunts came."

"Maybe these cunts're too fuckin' scared to go near the pub!" snorted another.

Some of the locals actually apologised for Fearman's pushy behaviour and we were even invited to stay and surf, but not to shoot. The locals then debated among themselves about whether or not we might be allowed to shoot some of the lesser-quality local waves, like Saltbush Point.

"Saltbush isn't a performance wave," replied Bill. "It's not worth shooting."

"Fuck, Vortex isn't a performance wave either," snorted Beardman. "It's just a fuckin' tube! What else is there to surfing?"

Saltman reluctantly interjected. "Ah ... these cunts were actually doing, uh ... other stuff out Vortex today."

"I don't fuckin' care if they were fuckin' doing ... I dunno, fuckin' ... reentries in the tube!"

Beardman's eyes almost spun.

Fearman, who'd been squatting by Ferg and calling him a "white black man", sparked up again. "I'm sick of fuckin' talking! We'll come back tomorrow and sort things out then."

I started to relax at last. But Fearman had a parting shot. It seemed he had learnt of our plans to travel to a remote island off the South Oz coastline.

"You cunts'll never get to Sealer Island!" he exploded from his ute. "There'll be a welcoming committee ready to stop you! We'll phone all along the coast, and they'll be ready and waiting for you at the airport ... with guns! So you cunts may as well leave this state, now!"

With that, the posse roared off into the night, and the desert wrapped itself in silence around us once again.

No-one spoke for a long time. We were all exhausted on every level. Finally, I croaked, "Let's leave, right now. Like Fearman said."

"But we won," said Garve. "They've gone."

"Yeah, they've gone back to the pub. But what happens when they've all had 20 more drinks? Imagine Fearman convincing his mates how easily we got off. They'll be back after midnight, when we're asleep, to ram home their point."

There was weary nodding. This was one argument I didn't need to press.

"Let's just leave this state," said Ferg.

"Let's leave Saltbush, anyway."

So we packed up the gear, and drove. At Saltbush town, we recognised Saltman's ute in the only petrol station, so we limped on, low on fuel, and on, until we came to a caravan park, far from the coast. By now, team resolve had returned and, with it, a plan. We all agreed not to be beaten. After phoning the caretaker on Sealer Island, an alternative, private airstrip was organised for our flight.

The groms still seemed dubious, until the caretaker pointed out that he owned a rifle, and was prepared to use it against any unwelcoming committee, not just against feral cows. So we backdoored Sealer Island the way we'd frontdoored Saltbush, and ended up with some screaming eight-to-10-foot barrels for Bill to photograph at last, and to add to our unphotographed memories of perfect Vortex.

* * * * * * *

A few afterthoughts:

The Saltbush crew proved they would go to any

lengths to discourage visitors from plundering their waves and media swine from exposing them. Yet on an all-time offshore day at Vortex, only two locals turned up, and one of them didn't even get wet.

It is possible that none of the Saltbush locals meant to kill us that night, or even to rough us up. They may well have intended only to scare us, in which case they succeeded magnificently, and are probably still chortling up phlegm today.

Maybe some of the locals even wanted us to stay, to see some progressive surfing, but those voices were so soft as to be inaudible that night.

Despite our differences, and my abhorrence for many of their methods, I still have a fundamental respect for the Saltbush locals. They have a system, a hierarchy, and it is enforced, albeit brutally. I'm sure there are many aggro wave-hog visitors who deserve whatever punishment the Saltbush locals mete out.

I envy the underground surfers from my home town who make regular pilgrimages to the desert, and who are as accepted and respected as any outsiders can be. Basically, they don't get worked over because they show respect for the local system, don't act like East Coast wankers, don't take any photos (or pro surfers), don't hit the surf in a frothing pack and never, ever pull back when called into a wave. Better by far to plunge over the falls and get totally smashed than be condemned for evermore by the locals as a pull-back cunt.

Personally, I regret that I have become something of a media demon incarnate to an entire state. I've been confronted on the beach as far away as South Africa and let known that I must never again cross the South Australian border (though the warning didn't stop me last time). If my words have led to more crowds, or an overall deterioration of the quality of surfing at Saltbush, then I am truly sorry, for that was never my intention.

I only hope the Saltbush locals will note that in all my articles about them, even in this potential get-square piece, I have not revealed the location of any South Australian surf spot, nor even once typed the true name of Saltbush (though, face it fellas, the joint is wound up in Australian surf legend almost as much as Bells or Margarets). Every surfer knows Saltbush, even if just in his or her soul. Most also know what a festering, inhospitable hole it is, a crucible of madness where Sigmund Freud could've written a large psychiatric volume, if he didn't die of lung cancer first, or wasn't ridden out of town on a rail. My words have hardly discouraged such outsider trepidation. If anything, I've acted as a sort of Saltbush anti-PR agent.

Despite all that, I know I will die a happier man if I can return to the desert before my surfing days are done, even if just once.

Double that for Bill Alexander. He didn't want to go to Saltbush with pro surfers in the first place, and he certainly didn't want me to write, "The Terror in the Saltbush" for *ASL*. "You'll just add fuel to the fire," he said, and he was correct.

Bottom line, sad for some. The Saltbush system works. Everyone must show respect or else. The goal of minimising surf magazine publicity has also worked magnificently. For the quality and range of its waves, the Saltbush stretch of South Australia receives less publicity than anywhere else in Oz (except maybe west Tasmania).

* * * * * * *

Postscript

The first Tubequest series proved very successful in building *ASL* a more core reputation. Yet the fortunes of the original Tubequesters have varied capriciously in the six years since we kicked the shit out of the unsuspecting Tubemobile ...

Despite remaining one of the finest lensmen in the country, Billy Alexander doesn't take many surf shots these days. Enjoying his family and helping protect the Central Coast environment rate more highly.

Mick Campbell set the surfing world on fire when he and best mate Danny Wills pushed Slater to the title wire in '98. With twice as many muscles as he possessed in '94, the Gingernator remains a prime world title contender.

Amazingly, though he dominated the photos in the first Tubequest spread, Jason Gava has done no magazine trips since Tubequest. A hard-working jack-of-all-trades, Garve can still be seen pulling in whenever his beloved Sandon Point is cranking.

Andrew Ferguson died in senseless circumstances in 1999. Though John Howard remains incapable of expressing sorrow to Ferg's people, the surfing world still mourns the loss of this incredibly talented young man.

BEATING THE DRUM

A guide to effectively resolving conflict in the line-up.

Gordon Stammers

45-year-old Gordon Stammers has lived and surfed on the west coast of Victoria for 25 years and has taught communication and anger management programs for 15 years with the State Government's Justice Department. He has recently completed a training manual for schools titled Sorting it out, a surfers' guide to resolving conflict in the line up. *A dedicated surfer and family man, Gordon feels passionately about the problem of Surf Rage and is doing everything he can to put an end to this disgusting practice.*

Barra da Tijuca, Brazil: a 37-year-old surfer slotted perfectly to enter a six-foot glassy tube is dropped in on and collides heavily with a young surfer. He becomes tangled dangerously in the grommet's leg rope and is dragged 100 metres down the beach under powerful white water. His head is smashed continually by the offender's surfboard, and upon surfacing is casually told by the grommet to "get fucked, ya old bastard". When challenged for his comments, the young grommet follows the older surfer to shore and the matter is settled with fists.

Malibu, California: a visiting surfer is set upon by an out of control local, he is taunted to fight and then ordered to "piss off outa here if you wanna live". His crime was to ask a local surfer to stop dropping in during an earlier surf session.

Angourie, Australia: one of Australia's most famous surfers, a tribal elder with a mischievous reputation, is hammered to a pulp in one of the nastiest bits of aggression ever role-modelled to the surfing youth of Australia.

International media coverage of the violent assault on legendary Australian surfer Nat Young widely promoted the view that today's surfers are more accepting of and give prestige to violent behaviour in the surf, where they once would not. Media commentators everywhere began referring to a deliberate attempt to hurt another surfer after a surfing-related incident as "Surf Rage" and suggested that violence in the world of surfing is rapidly on the increase.

If we examine the history of surfing from a world perspective we can see that many popular surfing locations have experienced lengthy periods of rising conflicts and misunderstandings. For instance, the inventions of leg ropes, wave skis and knee boards in the sixties, the boogie board in the eighties and the recent reemergence of the Malibu in the nineties all brought increases in both crowds and conflicts as popular surf breaks became intensely competitive environments.

Thankfully these unwelcome changes to the surfing environment were usually followed by a return to "a fair go for all" *according to their skill and ability in the water* (and as long as wave skis and boogie boarders stayed away from classic breaks on those classic days).

But now things are different, as more and more surfers (and other surfcraft users) in crowded surfing environments take greater risks to test their skills and lay claim to what they consider is their fair share of available waves. Intense competition and fighting for waves has become a way of life for many male surfers and, as one surfing elder said to me recently, "there now exists a bigger distance between the traditional 'Surfers' Code' and its day-to-day use than ever before".

Unfortunately, very little research currently exists on the numbers of surfers paddling around line-ups flexing their muscles while growling animal noises at all in their path. Thankfully though there is an enormous amount of information at our disposal that helps us form both reliable profiles of those surfers most likely to act violently in our surfing environment and also offers some very reliable strategies to increase personal power in the face of intense conflicts and strongly convey the message that violence in surfing is ugly and unacceptable.

Let's begin by examining American and Australian statistics, which reveal that those people most likely to commit serious violence in our society are males in their late teens to early twenties who have one or both of the following personality factors:

- a lack of empathy and sympathy for the suffering of others;
- an inability to delay one's impulses or feelings (especially in those with over-controlled personalities).

Other contributory factors include:

- being parented with physical punishment and threats (aggressive children tend to grow into aggressive adults);
- having previously been rewarded for behaving aggressively, i.e. being praised by peers or obtaining a desired goal;
- having witnessed their significant role models (mum, dad, relatives, peers) using aggression;
- poor communication and problem-solving skills.

If we take the above facts seriously, we surely cannot examine the issue of violence in surfing without taking a quick look at gender issues. Research studies in western society are continually showing that when females experience conflict or communication problems with others, they tend to talk out their problems and show their feelings in an effort to understand another's point of view and resolve differences.

Males, on the other hand, when experiencing hurt

or rejection usually become either defensive or aggressive and emotionally fragile when conflict arises and cope by throwing themselves into an activity of some kind. Males are not very good at talking about their problems and resolving conflicts effectively and this is surely evidenced in the proportion of assaults and violent acts attributed to males in western society today (80–90 per cent).

To show anger, a tough exterior and an emotionally closed-off attitude is still the norm for most men engaged in conflict. Men in western cultures are still using a limited emotional range to deal with conflict and often miss the chance to use pro social behaviours mostly identified with females.

With such striking differences in the way males and females generally resolve conflict, surely the increased presence of females in the surfing environment can only enhance positive communication in the line-up.

So with all of the above research at hand (including the obvious fact that males today dominate the sport of surfing from administration right through to numbers in the water), what measures can the surfing fraternity (that's you and me) take to ensure that surfing remains a vigorous and exciting sport without the fear of unnecessary aggression and violence?

An important place to begin is to examine your personal attitude towards resolving conflict and misunderstandings in the surfing environment. Do you honestly believe it's OK to abuse, threaten or inflict harm on others, or do you believe that all surfers have the right to express their feelings openly and honestly and feel safe in the water?

Next, you need to evaluate your toolkit of communication and problem-solving skills and truthfully ask yourself whether there is room for improvement and, if there is, whether you're prepared to make the sustained effort needed for change.

If you have determined there is room for improvement (and there always is), then it's a very short step to the learning of three proven and highly-successful communication skills that will, firstly, empower you to stand up for your rights in conflict (Assertive Anger); secondly, change the way you think and act towards others when angry (S.T.A.R.); and, thirdly, help you deal more effectively with a surfer's anger in the line-up (Active Listening).

So read on if you are a male surfer wishing to improve your relationships with others and take action to preserve social harmony in the surfing environment.

Assertive Anger
Before learning this particular skill you must realise that the expression of anger, if kept in its proper perspective and expressed appropriately, is a healthy activity. After all, it's a natural emotion designed to aid your survival and provide boosts of energy when you're most in need of protection or healing. Secondly, you must realise that *anger* (a feeling) is not the same as *aggression* (an action or behaviour), which is primarily designed to insult, hurt or cause personal injury to someone.

For this reason, your anger with another surfer during conflict is best expressed in a manner that is direct and non-threatening, yet still communicates your message effectively. This can be accomplished using the right choice of words framed as an "I" statement, which can easily be remembered as a three-part formula that simply describes:

1. THE BEHAVIOUR OR ACTION THAT MAKES YOU ANGRY (dropping in like that...)
2. HOW IT MAKES YOU FEEL (makes me mad or angry...)

3. WHAT YOU WOULD LIKE TO SEE HAPPEN
   IN THE FUTURE (so let me have the wave to
   myself next time).

Using "I" statements during conflicts with others ensures that you are hard on the *issue* (dropping in, etc.), yet soft on *surfer*.

The strength of an "I" statement lies in the fact that you are describing how a surfer's behaviour and actions make you feel, rather than how they personally make you feel and there's a very big difference in the conflict outcome when anger is expressed this way.

Here are examples of "I" statements:

- "Snaking my wave like that just gets me angry. Stop SNAKING ME."
- "Dropping in just gets me wild (frustrated etc,). Follow the code, mate, and don't drop in."

Make up "I" statements using the formula; just remember to keep them simple and to the point. Most importantly, remember to state how the surfing incident made you "feel", as bottling up your feelings will only interfere with your later ability to work out the problem and will prolong the conflict unnecessarily.

Some other tips for using "I" statements:

- *voice tone/volume:* use a neutral tone without being intimidating.
- *timing:* he/she who hesitates is lost, so express your anger and honest feelings as soon as possible after the event.
- *facial expressions:* let your expression speak the same language as your words. Don't smile nervously while expressing anger – a frown or displeased look is more appropriate.

Remember to save your "I" statements for those conflicts in the line-up that really matter and really stand a chance of being changed.

And while we cannot expect the skill of "Assertive

Anger" to work miracles in our crowded line-ups, we can predict, however, that the right choice of words when in conflict will inspire both your confidence and ability to sort out problems and bring positive changes to the way you are treated in the line-up. The next time you are in conflict and feel angry at being dropped in on, give "I" statements a go and see for yourself how effective they are.

STAR (Stop/Think/Act/Review)
The second strategy to use in situations of heavy conflict is the 10-second STAR technique, which is a four-step solution designed to cool you down when angry and help you problem solve the issue effectively.

It's very easy to learn – you simply say the word *Stop* in your mind when you start feeling angry during conflicts, take a long, slow, deep breath and repeat to yourself the words "*Calm Body, Calm Mind*".

You then *Think* as quickly as possible about the many different ways you can react to the surfer's action that has got you angry (you could use an "I" statement, you could smash him in the face, you could paddle away angry or you could also drop in later, possibly escalating the conflict into violence, etc.

You then *Act* by choosing the response that will bring the best outcome for you and the offending surfer. In most instances, this is to act assertively with an "I" statement, vent your anger effectively and resolve the issue firmly but fairly.

You then *Review* the situation later by examining the outcome of your decision. If it worked, keep using that response for other conflict. If it did not, try another response and review its success. Keep reviewing until you get the desired outcome and remember Alan Alda's famous line "Be fair with others, but then keep after them until they are fair with you".

The STAR technique is an easily remembered anger and problem-solving skill that, with practice, will help you manage your anger and resolve problems more effectively.

Active Listening
Now that you have learned skills to express both your anger effectively and speak up for what you want, it is time to learn a valuable skill that will help you deal with another surfer's anger more effectively.

Active Listening is a skill that helps you acknowledge another surfer's anger by checking for both meaning and content.

Using the right choice of words, you provide a mirror for an angry surfer to see their reactions more clearly, to feel understood and to calm down and deal more rationally with their problem.

The three parts of Active Listening are:
- Acknowledging the content – What is the issue here?
- Acknowledging the feeling – What are they feeling?
- Acknowledging the solution – What can prevent this problem in the future?

Here are two different examples of someone listening to an angry surfer's grievance. The first example reveals how most surfers today respond to angry outbursts from another surfer, while the second describes an Active Listening approach to the same conflict.

Firstly, imagine someone dropping in and causing a very nasty wipe out for the up and riding surfer:

Surfer A: What did ya drop in for, idiot? I was slotted for a perfect tube. I yelled out it was my wave. What the hell were you doing? You crazy?

Surfer B: Sorry mate, didn't see you.

Surfer A: You what? I was right inside. Don't give me that crap.

Surfer B: Hey. Things don't always go the way you'd like them to, buddy. That's life!

Surfer A: Bullshit. Do that again and you're a dead man.

Surfer B: I'm what?

Surfer A: You're a dead man, idiot – you hear me?

Surfer B: Look, if you can't handle it, get out of the water.

Surfer A: I should belt your head in.

Surfer B: Come on, buddy, bring it on then. Let's go, on the beach now, let's go.

Now compare the same conflict with the following changes in Surfer B's responses:

Surfer A: What did ya drop in for, idiot? I was slotted for a perfect tube. I yelled it was my wave.

Surfer B: I'm sorry. I misjudged that wave.

Surfer A: You what? Don't give me that crap. I was right inside, idiot.

Surfer B: I truly didn't see you until it was too late and I can understand your anger, mate.

Surfer A: Anger! How do you think I feel? That was a bitchin' wave and you stuffed it. You stuffed me up. Drop in again and you're dead.

Surfer B: I ruined your wave and I'm sorry. I'll be more careful in the future.

Surfer A: Just follow the surfers' code and don't drop in next time – or else.

Surfer A paddles away, maybe not 100 per cent happy, but content knowing that his feelings and complaints have been acknowledged by Surfer B.

As the second example demonstrates, not all surfing conflicts have to begin with name calling and end with hostile anger and aggression.

Remember, most surfing violence occurs between surfers who retaliate with put-downs and abuse. Refusing to get into a tit-for-tat with an out-of-control surfer and using the skill of active listening is the first step to staying safe and stopping the escalation of bad feelings.

Other Tips to Reduce Surfing Anger and Stress

Avoid hanging out with surfers who behave aggressively: their behaviour is contagious and detrimental to your mental health. If a close friend is behaving out of character and getting aggressive with other surfers, take the time to explore his feelings and find out what's bothering him. You may save him, or someone else, from unnecessary violence.

Give first time drop-ins who apologise the benefit of the doubt. However, act like a broken record with "I" statements if they continue to drop in – the message will get through. If you have dropped in or interfered with another surfer by accident, acknowledge your mistake honestly, actively listen to their grievance and apologise with dignity.

Don't rush your surfing by clocking the amount of waves you get. This type of surfing causes you to see any interferences in a negative light. Relax, enjoy the friendly competition for waves and use effective communication with those aggressive surfers having a bad day.

If you find you have strong feelings of rage during conflict and want to punch someone out, remember the STAR technique or try reframing the incident with phrases like: "He's obviously having a bad day, why should I take it personally and ruin my day?"; "Don't act like a jerk just because he is"; or "He looks out of control, so easy does it". If none of these self-talk statements work, leave the water, calm down on the beach and respect your good reputation.

On those busy days, have your surf a little earlier in the morning or later in the day to avoid the rush hours if possible.

Finally, remember that your angry thoughts and feelings are not really caused by other surfers or situations, but by the way you think about those people and situations. Nothing affects the way you approach a conflict more than your attitude and state of mind at the time. Your attitude also affects how much fun you have, how successful you are at achieving new manoeuvres and, most importantly, how much respect you receive from your peers in the line-up.

So if you are a male surfer faced with potential conflict in the water, next time think about your attitude and reactions, use your newly-learned skills and have a great day in the line-up, because the world needs more surfers like you right now.

Note

The information here is only a general guide to effective communication. Do not assert your rights with extremely aggressive surfers unless you are exceptionally confident in your communication skills and feel safe in doing so. If a violent, unprovoked attack is made on you and escape is not an option then saving yourself from injury by fighting back may be the best option.

If you wish to know more about assertive communication skills or anger management, contact your neighbourhood house or council social worker – they are sure to be able to put you in contact with an inexpensive communication program.

SURF RAGE

Nat Young

The conditions that will likely result if the negativity in the ocean continues to build are painful to imagine. Surely anything that can be done to defuse potential Surf Rage situations is a step in the right direction.

Here's an interesting one that's been around for a while.

One older surfer in my area has suggested that everyone should stop wearing a leg rope when surfing Angourie Point. This would certainly help spread the crowd, as no-one would be keen to take too many chances when they risked losing their board on the rocks. Before leg ropes were invented in the early '70s, a swim after your board every now and then was considered totally normal, something that happened almost every time you went for a surf and was not such a bad thing.

Swimming to the beach was how I learnt to body-surf competently. I also gained understanding about the shape of the reef and the power of the waves I was attempting to ride. I have observed that many kids today don't even know how to bodysurf. Some can barely swim.

The leash or leg rope has played a pivotal role in the changing reality of surfing. Unquestionably, leg ropes make surfing safer in crowded situations. At the same time, not wearing leg ropes could really help out at breaks like Angourie, where we get a lot of people jockeying for position. The problem is – at Angourie as elsewhere – people rarely see eye to eye on anything, let alone something as personal as the leg-rope issue.

Not even the better surfers, who rarely fall off, can agree to it. It's like trying to get Americans to give up their guns. So, nothing has happened and probably never will with this very worthwhile idea.

Tribal Law

On a more positive note, the first plaque inscribed with the Tribal Laws of Surfing has stood proudly amid an impressive pile of rocks at the main break at Margaret River in Western Australia since October 1998. Rosco Kermode, Peter Cuming, and my old friend Robert Conneeley in Margaret River have been working on this Tribal Law concept for many years.

No matter who you are, when you walk down the beach at Margaret's, it's right there in your face, before you even attempt to paddle out, reinforcing all the rules experienced surfers know but, unfortunately, sometimes seem to forget.

Credit is due to the local surfing community, which unanimously supported the erection of the bronze relief and has allowed it to remain. I have heard that some of the better surfers in the south-west of the state feel this display of the laws of surfing is unnecessary. The majority of the tribe, however, seems to believe that it does no harm, looks impressive, and is a positive step towards more enjoyable, safer surfing for everyone, not just the novice surfer.

It's an attitude thing, ofcourse. A plaque can't make anyone change the way they are. Surfers who are violent by nature will probably be violent until the day they die; they'll only change if they really want to. All the same, seeing the Tribal Laws on display gives everyone the opportunity to know what is and isn't acceptable behaviour at that particular break. It's safer and better if we all play by the rules.

After my assault, a television company in Sydney paid me $12,000 for an interview. That money is now being held in trust for *The Spirit of Surfing*, where it will be used for projects that will benefit the whole of surfing. *The Spirit of Surfing* concept was first put forward to me by surfing friend Peter Cuming in 1995. It involves us as surfers protecting surf environments, looking out for each other and celebrating the deep connection we have with the ocean and nature, no matter what our level of experience or skill. I hope that other surfers and companies will contribute something and that great things will happen.

The first project is placing Tribal Law plaques at as many breaks as we can afford. One of the prime movers, Rosco Kermode, is a true artist; his original depictions of surf spots are wonderful pieces of art that show the different breaks, the rips, and the land forms relative to the beach in the area.

If enough surfers feel that a relief of the Tribal Laws would be helpful at their beach, Rosco will go to that area and design the art to fit or assist local artists to do it. In short, *The Spirit of Surfing* can make it happen, but only if a majority of people surfing an area want it.

Getting local surfers involved is the real catalyst to the success of this or any other surf-related project. Before any new work begins, we make sure the energy for the plaques comes right from the surfing communities themselves.

So if you have a problem with Surf Rage in your area or you wish to let travelling surfers know of the local surfing customs and you think a plaque with Tribal Laws would help, write to us at Spirit of Surfing Trust, P.O. Box 510, Maclean, NSW 2463, Australia, and we will see what we can do.

The Spirit of Surfing

On the weekend of 11-12 June 2000, a group of surfers met in Byron Bay in northern New South Wales to discuss a wide range of issues concerning the deterioration of surfing's cultural traditions, specifically Surf Rage and the general lack of respect between and among surfers.

Some 40 surf elders came from a very broad spectrum of the surfing world.

There were surfboard builders, old professional surfers, doctors, environmentalists, filmmakers, coastal managers, teachers, promoters – all brought together by Ian Cohen, Australia's first surfing-minded state politician.

The group initiated the inaugural "Sprit of Surfing" conference and discussed a wide range of topics, including the psychology of anger, the social ecology of surfing, commercialisation, surfers and the environment, and communications.

Throughout the process of the gathering the group focused on practical outcomes and our core areas of concern.

These were:

- developing an educational package for surf schools and for kids in our regular schools as well;
- promoting responsible/ethical business practices within the surf industry and incorporating environmental and ethical considerations into the manufacturing and distribution of surf gear;
- inviting all sectors of the surf community to participate in a revival of the spiritual heart and culture of surfing, through coming together, communicating, and celebrating; and
- supporting a Spirit of Surfing Trust to facilitate communication and action between surfing's various groups in protecting and promoting the positive values inherent in the spirit of surfing.

Back to the Future

Since the end of the 1960s, when we discovered what a good wave was and how to ride it, the number of surfers has grown rapidly, way out of proportion to the amount of quality surf available. Maybe it was the media's discovery of our sport and all the accompanying publicity. Perhaps it was the rise of Quiksilver, Billabong, Gotcha, and all the rest that have enticed more and more converts to our sport. No matter how you look at it, we have a lot more surfers now than we did in the '60s (and it was already crowded then), and it's growing every day. More surfers. The same amount of waves.

Logic tells us that something has to give.

It has been reported that there is at least one surfer in every family in Australia. Indeed, official figures estimate over a million active surfers in Oz. These days it's not uncommon in both Australia and America to have third-generation surfing families, grandfathers surfing with their children and their children's children.

From my perspective, this is basically a good thing. Surfing makes for a more conscious society. The more people who get into surfing's underlying alternative values – from respect for the environment to understanding the laws of nature – the better. The fact is, there's no turning back the clock; the cat is out of the bag, so to speak, and you can't blame the newcomers for wanting to experience what some of us have had for the past 40 years.

Making Reefs

I believe that creating more waves is the best method of diffusing the volatile situation that exists in the surfing world today. Since the advent of leashes, although we are surfing more challenging breaks, waves that were considered impossible "close outs" in the past, the leash has also made it easier for more surfers to catch more waves. So, in essence, given that the same number of waves breaking year after year is finite, the ratio of surfers to the number of rideable waves has not significantly improved.

The most realistic method of making waves I have seen so far is artificial reefs, but on the whole the progress of this alternative seems painfully slow in bearing fruit. To my knowledge, the most successful man-made break presently being surfed on a regular basis is at Cottesloe in the Perth (Western Australia) metropolitan area. The WA government was very supportive of surfing, and development of the reef at the Cable Station was part of its election policy in 1993. A few years ago, several upwardly-mobile Perth surfing businessmen reminded them of their pledge – and presto! – the project was on. The design for the Cables artificial surfing reef was totally realistic; they would take the very average right-hander that broke only on rare occasions and build up a shallower reef that would deliver a fast peeling right on any swell.

The project was relatively expensive for the state government, costing over $A1.5 million and taking three months (over a couple of years) to complete the 120-metre-long, 50-metre wide reef. Large wire cages were filled with rocks; the parcels were then transported by barge and placed in exact position while the swell and wind were down. The project was considered totally complete in 1999; however, a number of local surfers would like to see the reef made shallower so the wave would break a bit hollower on smaller swells. Apparently this could be accomplished by laying sandbags in place over the rock form.

The swell component was the only problem with the Cables reef plan. Because of its position, sheltered behind Rottnest Island to the west and the off-shore reefs to the north, the Perth area does not receive much uninterrupted ocean swell. However, these days, when the swell is hitting the Cables artificial reef clean and square, the waves are fantastic – a vast improvement on what was there before.

Certainly it seems like sandbags are the answer for artificial reefs – big sandbags. In fact, 320 huge sandbags, each weighing 500 tonnes, are being used to create a surf break at Narrowneck on Queensland's Gold Coast. If the concept works, the Gold Coast City Council plans to build another seven sandbag reefs along the coast from the Tweed River up to Southport.

At Narrowneck, as with the Cables reef, a barge was used to manoeuvre the bags into position, but there the similarity between the two projects ends. The Gold Coast Council's plan was both to stabilise the movement of sand, which has been devastating the area's tourist industry for the past 25 years, and to build a high-quality right- and left-hand surfing break that would be the equal to any in the world. The right is the superior wave, but the paddling channel created between the breaks will produce a surfable left as well. At this time (June 2000), the $A2 million reef is not quite complete. New Zealand surfer and project designer Kerry Black says only 30 more bags are required to finish the job, but consistent high surf in recent months has put the project a bit behind schedule.

Making Waves

Apart from artificial reefs, the only realistic alternative for creating surfable waves is a system that I first experienced in Long Beach, California in February 2000: Wave Loch.

I first heard about the Wave Loch system in Hawaii in 1993, when Gerry Lopez told me about this perfect six-foot barrel he had been invited to try in Norway. "Norway?!" I was amazed. "Everyone knows there are no waves in Norway!" But Gerry said it was fantastic; he nearly got tubed. I tried to learn more, but information was sketchy at best.

But then came this year's Swatch Wave Tour, which was supposed to have been part of the Action Sport Retailers trade show. But ASR organisers feared the Swatch program would take attention away from the show, so they pulled away from the deal. In the end, Swatch made a deal with the owners of the huge, retired *Queen Mary* to set up on the lawn right next to the gracious old lady.

This is where I encountered the Swatch Wave, the world's first portable wave. The show pulled into town on the backs of 40 semi-trailers. Nine twelve-metre containers were bolted together to form the wave, pool and component machinery. It took 600,000 litres of Long Beach City water to fill the pool. A month earlier, this same Swatch Wave had been erected in the centre of Florence, blowing the minds of the Italians in Michelangelo's beautiful land-locked city.

On that first night in Long Beach, I was lined up with hundreds of people waiting to get in. I began to understand why ASR management feared the Wave Loch would overshadow the trade show. It was an awesome sight! The entire operation covered about the same area as a moderate-sized circus. The stadium had seating for 1,500 guests; it was packed to capacity. It seemed like such a contrast to me – state-of-the-art wave technology right next to a ship that conjures such nostalgic images of the last century.

Everything was so very professional – an announcer introduced the pro team, and, on cue, each surfer strapped on something that looked like a wakeboard-cum-snowboard and sat at the edge of the high-velocity stream of water that poured out of the jets and up onto the wave face.

I had goose bumps; it really was a perfect eight-foot tube. But it looked like it was strictly one rider on the wave at a time, and the team were all over it, until they cranked up the power, so that the tube became more intense, sucking the rider back down the throat; or they decided to ride off the back of the wave and into the still water of the pool.

All the professional surfers – both male and female – were very competent, either carving on the face or pulling back into the barrel, but only Christian Fletcher was spraying the crowd on every cutback, and they loved it! You could study the individual styles of the pros, just a few feet away, sort of like an extreme close-up. Rob Machado's unique tube-riding style was right there on display. I could actually analyse how he made it work – much more effective than any video I've seen.

I had to have a go myself, and the next night I did. It was as exciting as my first wave on a surfboard, and it didn't help when, minutes before, I saw Rush Randle actually break his arm when he hit the bottom after getting sucked over the falls. Everyone else was coming out unscathed, and all the nervous butterflies disappeared as soon as I actually pushed off. With a little guidance from Luke Eden, I managed to stand for a few seconds before disappearing backwards down the barrel. The next time was a bit better, and I made one halfway decent turn before getting wiped out. Each time I had a go my ability improved, and by the end of the show I could stay upright for a few turns.

Apparently, the first standing wave of this sort was built for a pool in Texas. The designer, a Californian named Tom Lochtefeld, created the thing after watching and riding standing waves on the Snake

River for years. He completed the first one in 1991. This Swatch Wave was actually another of Lochtefeld's, and when his contract was up with Swatch, Tom moved the whole deal to a permanent location in San Diego, where Wave Loch will open to the general public in July, who will pay on the basis of the actual time they ride.

The Lochtefeld Wave Loch is the best crowded-surf alternative I've seen so far. Since it does not need the ocean or swells, the mind boggles trying to imagine where this will lead over the next 20 years. Lochtefeld has now built four standing waves in pools around the world. However, at a price tag of $US2 million each, they aren't cheap. Then again, cheap is relative. It's not so expensive for the Sheik of Dubai, who now has two of 'em at his city's water park – one the standard six- to eight-foot tube I've described and the other a more docile design, built for beginners to learn how to surf.

I just hope that when those beginners join us in the line-up, they will be treated with respect, and that they, in turn, will respect us, who have surfed for years in a growing atmosphere of Surf Rage. Let's hope we can put it all behind us, like a collapsing curl.

Kicking Out

Naturally, it was the assault that I recently experienced that brought this book project to a head. But it really is much bigger than one incident.

Like most people who surf on a regular basis, I have witnessed a growing amount of Surf Rage. In the past few years, I have seen another surfer punched out by the same man who assaulted me. I've seen and heard numerous angry verbal exchanges between surfers over wave possession in the line-up.

Hopefully, we can do something about this violence. I have been the receiver and instigator of Surf

Rage and I sincerely hope that we can all do something about this violence. None of it reflects the true Spirit of Surfing. Surf Rage is an ugly reality to most surfers. We've ignored it for a long time. Now it's time we took a closer look at ourselves.